ENERGY
ENTREPRENEURS

ENERGY
ENTREPRENEURS

INSIGHTS & INSPIRATION
FROM SELF-STARTERS
IN BUSINESS
AND INDUSTRY

EARL HEARD AND BRADY PORCHE

BIC Publishing
P. O. Box 40166
Baton Rouge, LA 70835-0166
(800) 460-4242
www.bicalliance.com

Energy Entrepreneurs

First Printing

Printed in the United States of America

ISBN-13: 978-0-9768310-1-3
ISBN-10: 0-9768310-1-5

Printed by RR Donnelley
Harrisonburg, VA
Cover design and layout by
Denise Poché & Heather Abboud

Quantity discounts available. Dealer inquiries welcome.

This book is dedicated to a loving and forgiving God, who has given me and many others the strength to overcome adversity through faith, hard work and perseverance.

This book is also dedicated to those who have played a role in bringing peace, happiness and success to others by sharing their life lessons and experiences. Every person has a story to tell, whether it's a tale of triumph or tragedy, happiness or sadness, success or failure.

I would also like to give thanks to my wife Bodi, my daughter Dane, my son-in-law and partner Thomas Brinsko, and my wonderful grandchildren — Hannah, Mary and Michael — for inspiring me to be a better person. A special thanks to my family, friends and BIC Alliance partners, along with every entrepreneur, business owner, manager, craftsman and laborer who helped inspire me to hone my skills and share the lessons I've learned with others.

I would like to extend my deepest gratitude to Brady Porche, who conducted the interviews with all the individuals featured in this book and turned them into wonderful stories, and to the individuals themselves — Sonny Anderson; Tommy Barber (son of the late Claude Barber); Brooks Bradford Sr.; John Egle; Helen Hodges; Jon Hodges; Keith Huber; Dave Johnson; David LaCook; John McNabb; Bubba Nelson; Bob Parker; John Michael Paz; Nicky Prejean; Dewon, Roger and Curt Rankin; Forrest Shook; David Starkey; Bert and Thomas Turner; Ken and Shelia Vermillion; and Pete Vrettakos — for sharing their stories and insights. I also want to thank the families, friends and business associates who encouraged and inspired them to be successful and tell their stories to others.

Last but not least, I'd like to thank Heather Abboud and Denise Poché, who turned our vision into a finished product with their amazing design and layout skills, and the editorial staff of BIC magazine — Jamie Craig, Kaye Benham, Katie Macaluso and Susan Kern — for their help in proofreading and editing the text.

— Earl B. Heard, CEO & Founder, BIC Alliance

Contents

1   Introduction

7   R.L. "Sonny" Anderson, Anco Industries Inc. and
         Scaffolding Rental & Erection Service Inc.

15   Claude Barber, Plant Machine Works

25   Brooks Bradford Sr., Aimm Technologies

33   John Egle, Hub City Industries/Turbine Stimulation
         Technologies/Louisiana Marine Transportation

41   Helen I. Hodges, Separation Systems Consultants Inc. (SSCI)

49   Jon Hodges, Evergreen Industrial Services

57   Keith Huber, Keith Huber Inc.

67   Dave Johnson, Sparkling Clear Industries

75   David LaCook, FabEnCo Inc.

83   John McNabb, Growth Capital Partners

93   Raymond L. "Bubba" Nelson, Allwaste Inc. and Sanifill

101   R.E. "Bob" Parker, Repcon Inc.

111   John Michael Paz, Godwin Pumps

119   Nicky Prejean, Southland Fire & Safety Equipment

129   R. Dewon Rankin, HRI Inc.

135   Forrest Shook, NLB Corp.

141   David Starkey, Empire Scaffold

149   Bert Turner, Turner Industries

159   Kenneth and Shelia Vermillion, Glove Guard L.P.

167   Pete Vrettakos, Atlantic Industrial

175   The BIC Alliance: Past, Present and Future

187   50 Tips for Success in Entrepreneurship

191   Suggested Reading

195   What's Next?

201   Contact Information

INTRODUCTION

Webster's Dictionary defines "entrepreneur" as a person who organizes and manages a business undertaking, assuming the risk for the sake of profit. The book *Entrepreneurship for Dummies* states that an entrepreneur is someone who creates a new opportunity in the world of business and assembles the resources (i.e. money, people and organization) necessary to successfully exploit that opportunity.

In the mid-1700s, the world began what we commonly refer to as the Industrial Revolution, a time of social and economic change resulting from the replacement of hand tools by machines and power tools. Since the Industrial Revolution began almost 300 years ago, mankind has gone from the horse and buggy to the automobile, and from gazing at the stars to orbiting the earth and traveling to the moon. We've also learned how to capture and refine fossil fuels and turn them into products that fuel our automobiles and airplanes and provide energy that helps make life better for people all over the world.

The many people who turned their dreams of a better world into reality were visionaries, and by making their ideas come to life, they became pioneers to whom we all owe a debt of gratitude. *The Prize: The Epic Quest for Oil, Money and Power*, a book in which Pulitzer Prize-winning author Daniel Yergin tells the story of the energy business from prehistoric times up to the modern era, discusses the significant roles energy entrepreneurs like John D. Rockefeller, J. Paul Getty and others played in the evolution of the energy business around the world. As the industry grew globally, it spawned millions of jobs and entrepreneurial opportunities for further generations of visionaries, many of whom founded successful service companies that still operate today.

Most of the books written over the past 50 years about energy entrepreneurs are about people who explored and drilled for oil in the late 19th century and the early 20th century. There are some excellent books about other industry-related entrepreneurs, such as *Onassis: Aristotle and Christina*, by L.J. Davis, and *Anatomy of an Entrepreneur*, by Joseph J. Jacobs, founder of Jacobs Engineering. I've collected and read as many

1

books about successful entrepreneurs as I could get my hands on, from Rockefeller, Getty, Onassis and Jacobs to Donald Trump, Lee Iacocca and Walt Disney. There isn't a single one from which I didn't glean a lot of great information, but many of those books are only about one person and offer only the author's perspective. I've searched for a book that offers snapshots of many inspirational individuals, but haven't found one that focuses on entrepreneurs who represent various sectors of energy-related industries.

As my interest in energy-related entrepreneurship grew and my personal entrepreneurial endeavors began to bring a greater degree of success and prosperity, one thing became increasingly obvious — my mentors have rarely been the famous icons of the business world who were either dead or too busy for me to meet in person. They are the energy entrepreneurs who, while they may be lesser known, command just as much respect and, in many cases, are more influential to most of us than the icons. I can honestly say that I've learned as many valuable lessons from the energy entrepreneurs I've known personally and shared experiences with over the past 40 years as I have from the many books I've read.

While the legends of the past may inspire us and fuel our dreams, it is our present generations of entrepreneurs and experienced managers and craftsmen who share their life lessons and make our road to success easier. When I first envisioned this book over a decade ago, some of the folks I wanted to interview died before we could interview them. Others that I've wanted to interview have died while the book was in progress or have suffered health problems that left them incapacitated. Thankfully, the ones who have passed on shared their life lessons with their children and their most prominent protégés.

I've always said that there are several great ways to learn, but observing or reading about the achievements of others whom we know, honor and respect are among the best. Because my partner Thomas Brinsko and I believe strongly in the importance of mentor-protégé relationships, we have decided to re-invest a portion of our company's resources to sharing the things we've learned from others through all our publishing efforts. We believe there's something in this book for everyone, whether you're an aspiring entrepreneur or executive or someone whose job was created by an entrepreneur.

The people we've selected to feature in this book are not only successful entrepreneurs, they're also role models in business and industry. They hail from many different backgrounds. Some were raised in metropolitan areas, others were reared on farms in small towns. All have earned degrees from the school of hard knocks, and some have postgraduate degrees from prestigious universities on top of that. The sizes of their companies vary — some earn annual revenues of half a billion or more, and some are in the $3 million-$5 million range. Their companies represent many different facets of

Earl Heard, right, and partner Thomas Brinsko of the BIC Alliance are strong believers in the importance of mentor-protégé relationships.

industry-related work, including engineering, construction, specialty contracting, equipment manufacturing, fabrication, environmental consulting, safety, investment and merchant banking, and others. A common thread, however, unites them all — the willingness to work hard and assume risk in order to be successful, benevolent and, above all, happy. I salute each of them for their willingness to share their stories in order to help others write success stories of their own.

In Merrill Oster and Mike Hamel's book, *The Entrepreneur's Creed*, there is a chapter devoted to the philosophy of Bob Buford, founder and former chairman of Buford Television and author of *Half Time: Changing Your Game Plan from Success to Significance*, titled "Beyond Success to Significance." The best insight I gained from reading that chapter and Mr. Buford's book was that it's important to help others after we've achieved success of our own, hence the common title.

Like most entrepreneurs, success has not come easy for me. Since I first decided to take on the challenge of becoming an entrepreneur more than 25 years ago, I've experienced or witnessed firsthand many difficult setbacks, including business failures, bankruptcy, ridicule, addiction, betrayal, family turmoil and even near-death experiences. (Trust me — the life of an entrepreneur is not for those folks who prefer to live their lives in serenity and comfort. It's more of a rollercoaster ride than a merry-go-round.) But as I wrote in my first book, *It's What We Do Together That Counts: The BIC Alliance Story*, the ability to overcome adversity has brought my wife Bodi and I closer to God and one another and taught us lessons that have allowed us to be successful and at peace in this phase of our lives.

Now that we've achieved that for ourselves, we have vowed to devote our days left on God's earth to helping make life easier, happier and more successful for others in the workplace and at home. This book will be a large part of that effort, and we hope to publish future volumes. It's our own way of moving, as Mr. Buford says, beyond success toward significance. We hope that all budding entrepreneurs and others who have achieved success will do the same when they've crossed the threshold through which every dreamer and visionary aspires to walk.

A life of peace, happiness, success, respect, influence and benevolence is yours for the taking. We hope that by reading the stories that follow, you'll move closer to fulfilling that dream.

May God bless you and your family in all your endeavors.

Earl B Heard

R.L. "SONNY"
ANDERSON

Founder
Anco Industries Inc. and Scaffolding
Rental & Erection Service Inc.

In the late '80s, industrial service company entrepreneur and then-National Insulation Association (NIA) President R.L. "Sonny" Anderson was given the task of representing the association at an industry convention in Paris before a French delegation. On the day his presentation was to be given, he spent the entire afternoon in his hotel room studying an English-to-French dictionary. Despite the difficulty in learning a language the Baton Rouge, La., native had never spoken a word of in just a few hours, Anderson was able to put together a speech and deliver it that evening.

To his surprise, the crowd applauded. But Anderson could only bask in the glory for a few moments.

"I go to sit down with my wife June, and she looks at me and says, 'They didn't understand a word you said.'"

This humorous occasion marked one of the few instances in Anderson's life in which he failed to communicate effectively with other people. Over the course of his career, he has built strong bonds with colleagues and customers alike. All of those bonds were important to the success of his companies — Anco and Scaffolding Rental & Erection Service, along with their many subsidiaries. A few, however, were absolutely vital — he was only able to found his first company after receiving a loan from a colleague with whom he'd formed a close friendship.

"One of the things that's helped me to grow and prosper in my career is that the friends I've made in business have been very willing to help me," Anderson said. "Every one of them trusted me. I think faith and trust in other people are the two main ingredients that you can attribute success to."

Success has come in large supply to Anderson, but it has never been easy. Like many entrepreneurs, he's faced his share of trials over the years. Few people who owned or managed energy industry-related businesses during the oil and gas bust of the early '80s have fond recollections of that period. Many entrepreneurs lost everything they owned, and only a handful were able to keep their businesses running and ultimately prosper when the industry recovered.

Perhaps the reason Anderson and his team lived to see the daylight after the storm was that he'd already experienced a number of setbacks by that time. With more than two decades of experience as a business owner, Anderson had seen work come and go, but he never lost his nerve when times got tough.

Perseverance is a quality he inherited from his father, a traveling salesman who was educated at home by his mother and never attended a formal school. His father always worked hard to provide for his family, no matter how challenging things were at any given time. (Anderson also had three older sisters — Francille, Betty and Jane — who played a major role in his upbringing.)

Anderson drew inspiration from reading his father's will, which he wrote on an old order form for produce before he died at age 91.

"It was just a one-page will," Anderson said. "It said, 'Son, I don't have much money left, but I hope it will be enough to bury me with.'"

Anderson's father likely had great faith in his son's ability to make his own life the best it could be, despite his humble upbringing. But the fact that he was born into a family that valued hard work, humility and courtesy more than personal wealth likely played the greatest role in Anderson's development and eventual flowering as a determined leader with a knack for endearing himself to people from all walks of life.

* * *

Anderson was born in Shreveport, La., in 1928. As a youth, he worked at a local bank, first as a filing clerk and ultimately as a teller. He began studying accounting and engineering at Centenary College, but left shortly afterward to take a job with Aber Co., an insulation company owned by his wife's uncle.

Anderson began working at Aber's Shreveport office as an estimator, and was promoted to branch manager not long afterward. In the mid-'40s, Anderson's boss made the decision to move him to Houston, which was on the cusp of becoming an epicenter for industrial activity. He spent a few years there, taking up residence in a YMCA building, but was moved back to Shreveport after the death of Roy Harrison, who had been running the company's branch office there.

In 1951, Aber sales representative Gus Maxwell opened a company branch office in Baton Rouge. Shortly afterward, Maxwell moved back to Houston, and Mr. Aber chose Anderson to run the Baton Rouge operation.

Over the course of his career, Sonny Anderson has owned or founded more than 30 companies and been heavily involved in industry organizations.

According to Anderson, the move to Baton Rouge was initially a daunting prospect.

"At the beginning it was just me, a girl and a warehouse," he said. "It was kind of hard at first because I was very young and didn't know anybody in Baton Rouge."

Faced with the task of running a new division in an unfamiliar place, Anderson worked hard to establish contacts at the local refineries. But as he built a name in the area for himself and the company, he began to lose contact with the home office in Houston.

"Houston was really beginning to grow," Anderson said. "The only time I'd see Mr. Aber was when he'd call a meeting. After those meetings, everyone would just return to their branches."

While working with Enco (now ExxonMobil) in Baton Rouge, Anderson became acquainted with an Enco purchasing agent by the name of Budd Anderson. During a meeting, Anderson expressed to Budd his apprehensions about his future with Aber.

"Budd said to me, 'Why don't you try going into business on your own?,'" Anderson said. "I said, 'I don't have any money.'"

Budd then encouraged Anderson to try to obtain the $12,000 in Aber stock he owned and borrow whatever else he would need. Anderson followed his advice, obtaining the stock and borrowing an additional $8,000 from Charlie Hogg, who was employed by a mechanical contractor with whom Anderson had previously worked.

On November 22, 1962, Anderson founded Anco with, as he says, "a hope and a prayer" that it would be a success. Having already made good contacts in the Baton Rouge area, Anderson and several employees (including Harold Johnson and Geneva Ivey, who would remain with him until the year 2000) hit the ground running.

"The business really picked up, and we started to grow," Anderson said.

The period from 1962 to 1969 was marked by consistent growth as Anco built and maintained relationships with plants across South Louisiana. In 1967, Anderson founded Scaffolding Rental & Erection Service, which was the very first company to specialize in the rental and erection of scaffolding for industrial contractors.

By the end of 1969, however, labor strife in the Baton Rouge area caused many plants to terminate contracts with service companies.

"During that time, we were forced to pull back and see where we stood and in what direction we would go," Anderson said.

Anderson and his team began to look at other markets for work, including Mississippi and Alabama. Meanwhile, the lack of local business made the task of sustaining Anco and its employees a constant struggle. Anderson, along with his wife and four children, owned a 108-acre plantation home in St. Francisville, La., that they were forced to sell just to keep the company afloat. The situation deteriorated to the point where Anderson was forced once again to rely on the kindness of a friend in order to pay his employees.

"I told Ray Marchand about the payroll situation, and he just asked me, 'Well, what do you need?,'" Anderson said. "I told him that I would need about $70,000. So, he drove me to his bank in Plaquemine,

10

La., and asked the president of the bank what he had available. The president told him that the only thing Mr. Marchand had that hadn't been loaned against was his farm. So, Mr. Marchand put his farm up and signed a note for me."

The labor crisis simmered in the early '70s, and business began to pick up again. By the end of the decade, Anco had formed several subsidiaries that offered specialty services like coatings and refractory work. As the company branched out into additional geographic regions, Anco's work force became more mobile. Airplanes were purchased to transport managers and engineers to and from jobs in places like Florida and North Dakota.

> *"I don't think I'd be where I'm sitting right now if I had no faith in my people. You can't do it all by yourself. You've got to treat your employees well."*

Anco flew high in those days, but turbulence soon came with the decline of the oil and gas industry and the rise of interest rates, the latter of which made equipment financing burdensome. The trials of the '80s, however, were not limited to those caused by turmoil in the energy business. A bank in which Anderson had invested significant personal assets began to experience financial problems.

"I had about 68,000 shares of stock in that bank, and it went to zero," Anderson said. "It was taken over by the federal government."

As if that weren't enough, the Anderson family was stricken by tragedy.

"At about the same time, we discovered that my wife had cancer," Anderson said.

In order to offset the cost incurred in the aftermath of the bank's collapse, Anderson sold Scaffolding Rental & Erection Service to Brand Services in 1989. This also allowed Anderson more time to spend with his wife as she began to undergo treatment for her illness. Although things would eventually return to normal at Anco, June Anderson lost her battle with cancer in 1992.

As Anco recovered and grew in the '90s, Anderson began to feel as though the company had lost the intimacy it maintained during its formative years. After much deliberation, Anderson made a tough decision about the future of his business that he knew would impact his life in a significant way.

"It was getting harder to hold everybody together at that time," Anderson said. "So, when the opportunity came along, we sold the business."

Anco was sold to United Scaffolding in 2000, ending a long chapter in Anderson's life as an entrepreneur. By that time, he was revered in the industry, having gained a reputation as a trailblazer for kick-starting the scaffolding business and as a source of inspiration for any entrepreneur who's faced adversity. Over the years he has returned the favors granted to him by his benefactors by assisting budding entrepreneurs.

Anderson claims to get great pleasure out of helping people achieve their dreams. That's not hard to believe considering that he's built a hugely successful career on the principle of keeping relations with clients, colleagues and employees as healthy as they could be.

* * *

Anderson, center, has been a mentor and a benefactor to many entrepreneurs, including Earl Heard, left, of the BIC Alliance. Also pictured is Ronnie Bourgeois, who has worked with Anderson for more than 40 years.

Today, Anderson operates Mechanical Insulation, a holdover from his previous company that he retained in order to keep together a core of colleagues — including Ronnie Bourgeois, who has worked closely with Anderson for more than 40 years. When the non-compete agreement Anderson signed with the purchaser of Anco expired in 2005, he and some of his former employees founded a new specialty contracting company called CSI. The new company is involved in major jobs in the Gulf Coast region, including the rebuilding of the areas affected by Hurricanes Katrina and Rita.

"I don't think I'd be where I'm sitting right now if I had no faith in my people," Anderson said. "You can't do it all by yourself. You've got to treat your employees well, which we've always done."

Not only does he possess the ability to get the most out of his team members, he also has a keen eye for talent, dedication and conscientiousness.

"Good employees are the best asset any company can have," Anderson said. "I read an article the other day that said to hire the wrong person costs three times his salary."

It would be easy for Anderson to rest on his laurels at this point in his career. Having built many successful companies from the ground up and served as a mentor to countless business owners, employees and other peers in industry, the recently remarried Anderson could justifiably retire to his Baton Rouge home and spend time hunting, attending sporting events or visiting with his wife Linda, his four children (both his sons, Patrick and Daniel, work in industry; his daughters, Beverly and Joni, are involved in other ventures) and 10 grandchildren. Giving up, however, has never been an option for him, and that's not likely to change anytime soon.

Although he put his college career on hold more than 50 years ago, Anderson has enrolled in the construction management program at Louisiana State University and is working toward earning a diploma (perhaps the only thing he hasn't achieved in life thus far).

"My goal is to get a degree before I die," he said.

In the meantime, Anderson is still the same hands-on manager he was when he first founded Anco in the early '60s. His team of managers expect early-morning phone calls from him each day, often times before the sun rises. Prior to that, however, he begins the day with a quick review of his priorities, along with an affirmation of his core principles.

"I keep a book in which I write down my to-do list," Anderson said. "I always say a prayer in the morning, whether I think it helps or not, and I vow to myself that I'll be sincere in telling people what I'm going to do."

More than anything, keeping promises to himself and his employees and customers has put Anderson in a comfortable position, one in which he can continue to do that which he loves — run successful companies — and take the time to make the decisions that will best enhance the remainder of his professional and personal lives.

He doesn't know much French, but Sonny Anderson has always spoken the language of entrepreneurship.

CLAUDE
BARBER
Plant Machine Works Inc.

About three years ago, Tommy Barber decided to end his 15-year career as a high school basketball coach.

As anyone who's worked in that profession knows, it can induce as much stress as almost any job imaginable. The task of training teenagers to focus on anything other than school and social activities is almost certainly an ongoing challenge. The work of Tommy's father Claude — who had purchased the Baton Rouge, La., equipment repair and fabrication shop Plant Machine Works in 1976 and grown it into a hugely successful, multifaceted operation — seemed favorable by comparison.

At least that's what Tommy thought in one pivotal moment during his final days on the court.

"My dad, believe it or not, never missed a basketball game that I coached," Tommy said. "Whether it was a home game or on the road, and whether or not my son Travis played, he was at every game."

During one particular contest, Tommy happened to peer across the gym and spotted Claude sitting proudly in the stands, just as he had at every other game of his son's long career. It was no special occasion, but for Tommy, this short glance was something of an epiphany.

"I said to myself, 'You know, I really should go and help him out,'" Tommy said. "Sure enough, within three weeks of that, I was done with coaching."

Tommy's lifelong dream was to coach basketball at the collegiate level. Shortly after retiring from the high school coaching scene, he received job offers from two universities. Even though they were the first

15

college jobs he had ever been offered, Tommy rejected both without giving either one a second thought.

This undoubtedly took Claude by surprise. Up to that point, his son had expressed no desire to work for Plant Machine Works in any capacity, though Tommy always had great respect for Claude's business. The chances of a Barber taking over Plant Machine Works after Claude's retirement — whenever that would be — appeared slim.

Tommy's change of heart, however, allowed Claude, his son and his management team to develop a five-year succession plan. The main objective was to have Tommy managing the day-to-day operations of the company while Claude handled sales and finances. In the meantime, Tommy would learn all the aspects of the business.

In September 2005, fate brought that plan to a screeching halt. Claude Barber, the heart and soul of Plant Machine Works, a man of great character and personality who had touched the lives of nearly every employee, customer, colleague and friend with whom he'd been associated, was diagnosed with brain cancer. Just four months later, he was gone.

To say Claude's illness was a wake-up call for everyone at Plant Machine Works is an understatement. Although he had a trustworthy and experienced management team and a hard-working crew of shop employees, a Plant Machine Works without Claude Barber was hard for anyone to imagine. Everyone in the company, including those who had been there more than two decades, had followed his lead every step of the way.

As was his style, however, Claude didn't fret over the future of his business when he became ill. He'd had his share of problems in his 29 years of owning Plant Machine Works, including economic downturns, employee betrayals and the myriad job- and customer-related mishaps inherent in any functioning business.

According to Tommy, Claude dealt with his illness like any other challenge — he handled it and moved on. The two men spoke every day during those final four months of Claude's life. In every conversation, Claude urged his son to not only be himself and make his mark on Plant Machine Works, but also to trust the management team that had worked so hard to keep the company successful — Estimator and CAD Specialist Kirk Jones, Customer Service Manager Eddie Hood, Shop Superintendent

16

Bobby Williams and Sales Manager Chad Laurent.

Tommy has heeded his father's advice. At the time of this writing, he had been at the helm for almost a year. Every day brings a new set of challenges, and Tommy readily admits that the growing pains have been constant. But Plant Machine Works is as strong as ever, though it will never be quite the same.

"They broke the mold when they made that man," Hood said of Claude Barber. "There was no one like him."

* * *

Claude was born in Baton Rouge in 1943 and raised there by his loving parents — Claude, a body man for a local car dealership, and Evelyn, a homemaker. He graduated from Istrouma High School and went on to study engineering at Louisiana State University. After college, Claude went to work for Yaun Manufacturing Co. as a draftsman and engineer trainee. In 1966, he was promoted to chief draftsman. The following year, Yaun was purchased by Anvil Industries. Claude was named chief engineer, a transition that set the stage for his eventual promotion to president and general manager.

During his time at Yaun, Claude met a businessman named Carmina, who opened Plant Machine Works in 1964 as a machine shop repair service for petrochemical companies. At the time he met Claude, Carmina was looking to retire. Claude saw great potential in Plant Machine Works, and worked out a deal with Carmina in which the latter would finance the former's purchase of the company over a set period of time. By 1977, Claude and his team — which consisted of his wife Linda and four other employees — were off and running. In just two short months, the new team tripled the company's existing business.

Integral to the company's quick expansion was the institution of new systems for doing business. But the real driving force was the sales acumen of Claude, who possessed a talent for engaging people and had built a broad network of contacts during his years at Yaun and Anvil.

According to those closest to him, Claude never met a person he didn't like.

17

"He was one of those guys where, within five minutes of meeting him, you felt like you'd known him all your life," Tommy said. "Everybody loved him."

"He was one of my very best friends," Jones said. "He was a pillar, and he always had my back."

Throughout his career as an entrepreneur and a manager, Claude made it a point to get to know his employees and customers at the personal level. His cherished bonds with his team members — many of whom had no qualms about sharing many aspects of their personal lives with the boss — instilled a sense of loyalty that allowed Plant Machine Works to thrive even during its toughest times.

Claude Barber purchased the Baton Rouge, La., equipment repair and fabrication shop Plant Machine Works in 1976 and grew it into a hugely successful, multifaceted operation.

"Claude was the best boss I ever had or ever will have," Laurent said. "I could approach him with any problem or situation and he always had time to listen and give his opinion or advice. You always walked away feeling that he really cared about you as a person, not just as an employee."

Similarly, Claude's steadfast determination to treat every customer, whether it was a multinational corporation or a small local business, with the same level of respect facilitated long-term business relationships.

"You didn't have to have the Exxon name to get help around here," Hood said.

"If he went into a plant and met the site manager and the floor sweeper, he'd greet both men the same way," Williams said. "That was his personality, and it's what made him successful."

In the early days, Claude worked his fingers to the bone performing all the important functions in the company.

"Mr. Barber used to do it all," Hood said. "He did the drafting, the purchasing and the estimating, and he drove a delivery truck."

Under Carmina, Plant Machine Works worked almost solely for

Exxon in Baton Rouge. That simple business model held up until the early '80s, when the local economy imploded and area businesses began cutting service and repair expenditures. Faced with the dilemma of either succumbing to the pressure or riding out the storm, Claude made the bold decision to diversify the business. In an era when many companies were either cutting back their work forces or going out of business altogether, Claude hired more people and buckled down for a period filled with uncertainty and 16-hour work days. It was around this time that Jones, Hood and Williams joined the company.

Plant Machine Works began serving a variety of new markets dur-

> ## *"I can't stress enough the importance of honesty with your customers, vendors and employees."*

ing the period of diversification, including grain, utilities, marine, pulp and paper, and government entities.

The gamble paid off immensely — after a brief period in which Claude was required to cut work hours from 40 to 32, Plant Machine Works rebounded in a big way. The company doubled and, ultimately, quadrupled its business over the next 15 years.

Claude reflected on that difficult period during an interview with BIC magazine in April 2001.

"There have been tough times along the way, but the spirit of teamwork here at Plant Machine Works has seen us through," Claude said. "We have worked hard, and we have established loyalty and trust, not only to the employer, but to the employees as well. We have always treated our customers and our vendors fairly and have followed a strict policy of honesty and integrity."

Just five months after Claude uttered those words, he faced what was perhaps the most emotionally wrenching episode of his career. The terrorist attacks of Sept. 11, 2001, hampered America's economy as quickly as the Twin Towers of the World Trade Center fell, and that trickled down to the industries served by Plant Machine Works. For the first time in the history of his company, Claude — the consummate people person — was forced to lay off workers.

"The economy was pretty bad that year to begin with," Jones said. "But Claude would not lay anyone off. He managed to keep everyone working 40 hours per week. When 9/11 came, however, everything fell off to nothing. We laid off as few people as we could without crippling the company, and it really hurt him."

"He had to let people go who had been here for 10, 15 and 20 years," Tommy said. "He even had to let go of some family members who were working here at the time. It just tortured him."

Faced with yet another period of instability, Claude had little time to grieve over the layoffs. Just as he had in the early '80s, he refocused and overcame the setback the only way he knew how.

"When things would get slow around here, he'd just go out and make sales calls," Tommy said. "And all of a sudden, work would start coming in the door."

Claude's approach to sales showed everyone who witnessed it that there was no real formula, nothing that could be taught in a textbook or a course at a university. What he possessed was a rare combination of mental toughness and people skills that's hard for one to acquire if it's not in the DNA.

"He overcame everything just by being Claude Barber," Tommy said.

* * *

Being Claude Barber was about more than just working hard and building relationships with clients and employees. He treasured time spent with his two sons, their families and, of course, his wife Linda. When not fishing at their False River home with their children and grandchildren, Claude and Linda would follow LSU's overachieving sports teams in their championship pursuits.

Tommy described two occasions in which Claude's passion for LSU sports led to long-lasting bonds with people he never would have met under ordinary circumstances. Both instances are indicative of the effect

20

Claude had on everyone who knew him.

"He went to Omaha, Neb., for the college baseball World Series one year," Tommy said. "He ended up meeting a group of guys, and they all hung out together for the entire week. My dad gave one of the guys his business card before he left."

The following year, that man called Claude and offered to pay his way to the World Series for no other reason than his desire to reunite the fun-loving Louisianan with his crew.

In 2005, the LSU women's basketball team advanced to the Final Four. Claude and Linda made the trip to Indianapolis to cheer on the Lady Tigers.

"They sat next to a couple from Texas at the first game," Tommy said. "They ended up spending the entire week with them. They went home, and then a few months later my dad became ill. Those people showed up at his funeral."

Tommy wasn't too surprised. After all, approximately 1,500 people attended the weekday ceremony, some coming from as far away as Tennessee.

"A lady came up to me and introduced herself and said, 'Tommy, I only met your dad for five days, but he had an impact on my life like no one else.' They felt obligated to come down here and pay their respects."

So how does one fill the shoes of a man whose inspirational power seemed limitless, even after his death?

For Tommy, the answer is simple. You don't.

"There's a lot of pressure in being Claude Barber's son," he said. "I have graciously accepted not being 'Tommy Barber.' I will always be 'Claude Barber's son.'"

Tommy agrees with Jones's assertion that he isn't quite the salesman his father was.

"No," Tommy said. "Nobody is."

Nor does Tommy have an entrepreneurial background. Jones, however, offered some perspective.

"You've got to look at it this way," he said. "When Claude took over the company, he didn't have a lot of that experience either. It's just something you acquire over time."

Tommy, however, has acquired many important managerial skills over the course of his brief career at Plant Machine Works. Most have been earned the hard way.

"You had better be able to deal with people," Tommy said. "You've got to get thick-skinned in a hurry because if you don't, people will eat you up and spit you out. Some people just live to intimidate or take advantage of you."

Tommy knows from some of his father's experiences the perils of being too kind. But those moments were also instructive in that they showed Tommy that people who commit acts of betrayal should be forgiven, if not trusted.

"He gave almost to a fault," Tommy said. "He took chances on people, and there have been some who took advantage of him. He was burned by it, but he never held any ill will. He would just say, 'That's life,' and move on."

Grace under pressure is a vital part of Claude's legacy. As Tommy now knows, the constant headaches that are symptomatic of running a business can wear a man down if he doesn't learn to deal with them in an appropriate manner.

"No matter what business you're in, there are customers who will tear you up even though you've done the job exactly the way they asked you to," Tommy said. "And you'll have employees who whine and complain about the wind blowing. You have to be willing to take some abuse, but at the same time say, 'I see where you're coming from, and I'm going to help you.'"

Compassion was perhaps the most important quality handed down by Claude to his son and his colleagues. Jones, Hood, Williams and Laurent recite the company line of treating all customers equally as if it were the first thing they heard as they walked through the front doors of Plant Machine Works, while Tommy illustrates his father's infinite kindness through anecdotes.

"I had an awning put on my house recently," Tommy said. "The owner of the awning company came over to my house to talk to me about what I wanted. He saw 'Plant Machine Works' written on my shirt and said, 'I knew a guy named Claude Barber over there who was my first customer 10 years ago!'"

The man, who ran into Claude during lunch one day and recognized him as a classmate from high school, went on to explain how Claude requested a 12-foot-by-12-foot tent upon learning about his new venture. It was just one of many instances in which Claude helped a small entrepreneur — even though he didn't really need the tent.

"He did things like that for people all the time," Tommy said. "He would be in the grocery store, and would see two kids standing at the counter and buy them a pack of gum. That's just the way he was."

"Claude was the best friend anyone could hope for," Laurent said. "He was always the first one to offer his support when he heard of someone in need. In a world full of 'me-first' people, he always considered the needs and feelings of others first."

* * *

The future of Plant Machine Works is bright. Jones, Hood, Williams and Laurent are happy to be working with the son of their mentor, and Tommy trusts the men as though they are members of his family. Future expansion is a possibility, but for now, the company is busy enough maintaining the status quo as it adjusts to life without Claude, who would surely be proud of the job his son and management partners have done.

"Sometimes I'll be reviewing financial records and wonder why a certain number is the way it is," Tommy said. "It may take me three hours to solve the problem, but I know that if he was sitting right behind me, he'd solve it in 30 seconds. I no longer have the luxury of him being here to solve those kinds of problems, but that's what is so good about having the other guys here. They help manage the day-to-day operations of the company, and that gives me more time to focus on other things, like health insurance."

Claude imparted many lessons about sales, customer service and business management before he left this

Plant Machine Works' current management team includes Kirk Jones, Chad Laurent, Tommy Barber, Eddie Hood and Bobby Williams.

23

world.

"I believe everyone should be encouraged to follow their goals, but they should remember a few things to help them along," he said in 2001. "First, don't be afraid to make decisions. Second, I can't stress enough the importance of honesty with your customers, vendors and employees. Last, and perhaps most importantly, work as a team, because we all work for the common good of each one of us."

His true legacy, however, lies in the way he lived and the path he took to success. He was a man of great faith with a strong commitment to excellence and a generous spirit.

"My father was proud to call himself a Christian," Tommy said. "With all that he had going on — running a business, training me and being the head of our family — he still found the time to serve as book-keeper and sound man for False River Baptist Church."

Claude treated everyone with respect, regardless of who they were, or what they owned, or how many times they may have wronged him in the past.

While no one will ever be Claude Barber, those who follow his example will surely find themselves in a position to emulate his success. Plant Machine Works stands as a living monument to his work. His story is an enduring testament to how one can enrich his life by staying true to himself and by bringing joy to the lives of others.

BROOKS
BRADFORD SR.
CEO & Chairman of the Board
Aimm Technologies

The fear of failure is a powerful and often detrimental influence. It can cause us to crack or perform below our expectations in high-pressure situations. It can prevent us from taking the first steps toward achieving a goal or trying to improve our lives. But it can also motivate us to work harder and more efficiently to reach an objective.

When it manifests itself in ways that lead to counterproductive behaviors, the fear of failure is extremely difficult to overcome, even for the most determined and resilient individuals. An asset common to successful entrepreneurs, however, is the unique ability to neutralize that fear through positive thinking and hard work. Without those two character traits, no aspiring entrepreneur can expect to succeed.

After graduating from the University of Texas with a degree in international finance in 1968, Angleton, Texas, native Brooks Bradford went to work for himself and never looked back. Having grown up on his family's farm in Angleton, Bradford already possessed the work ethic necessary to strike out on his own. Most importantly, he did not envision failure.

"I've always worked for myself, and it's never crossed my mind that I wouldn't succeed," Bradford said. "I guess that's the mindset of the entrepreneur, and you either have it or you don't."

Bradford moved to Houston right after college to find his opportunity.

"Houston was and still is a place where you can go and not run into any socioeconomic barriers," Bradford said. "If you worked hard and had good ideas, there were people who would give you a chance. Many of them would give you a second chance if things didn't work out the first time around."

He didn't have many other options — his father would not allow him to spend the rest of his life working on the family farm.

"I told my father I wanted to be a rancher," Bradford said. "I'll never forget his response. He said, 'Brooks, I didn't spend $10,000 getting you an education at the University of Texas so that you could move back to Angleton.'"

Young and energetic, Bradford began a career in real estate and was successful almost immediately.

"Sales seemed to be the quickest way for an energetic young man to make money, so I began as a real estate broker specializing in corporate franchise locations on the west side of Houston," Bradford said. "This was a good economic climate for growth, and I was fortunate to be in a position to take advantage of a great market. I worked exclusively on a commission basis and it never occurred to me that I needed additional education or training. Perhaps I could have become a better or more professional salesperson if I had worked for a large real estate company, but I was in a hurry to prove to my mother and father that I could achieve success at an early age."

After five years as a broker, Bradford moved into real estate development, specializing in small offices and warehouses. The real estate development business led him to owning and operating banks, and he later moved into industry. His true success story began when he purchased Mobile Air, a temporary refrigeration company based in Galveston, Texas, in the late '70s.

Brooks Bradford's true success story began when he purchased Mobile Air, a temporary refrigeration company, in the late '70s.

"Being a bank stockholder

26

allowed me to make myself available for various opportunities that arose," Bradford said. "I received a call from a friend at a large Houston bank who asked that I assist him in evaluating loan collateral on Mobile Air. The company had good service and management, but the documentation for the bank and the company was poor. Within a few weeks of consulting with the company's owners — Jack Kivich and Billy Lambert — I was able to make the bank and the company comfortable with each other. In addition, I recognized that Mobile Air could be an excellent service company with additional management and financing. I negotiated the purchase of 50 percent of the corporate stock, and within a few years purchased 100 percent of the outstanding stock."

Mobile Air was relatively small at the time of the purchase, but it didn't take long for Bradford and his team to grow it into the largest temporary refrigeration company in the world.

"All of the business skills that I had developed up to that point in my life came into play," Bradford said. "Marketing, sales, people skills, management and financing relationships were integral. In an 11-year period, our growth and profits were excellent."

Bradford attributes the quick success to the uniqueness of what Mobile Air had to offer, as well as a new approach to marketing.

"I think you have to have some sizzle on the steak," Bradford said. "You need to have a process or perform some method of work that's unique in terms of cost effectiveness and timeliness. With Mobile Air, there was no one doing temporary refrigeration at the time, so we manufactured 80-90 percent of the equipment. It was very capital-intensive."

As time went by, major manufacturers expanded into temporary refrigeration, making for an intensely competitive business environment. In 1986, Bradford sold Mobile Air to a major European company called Aggreko and set out to begin his next venture.

* * *

The search for a new growth company led Bradford to several very interesting, educational and profitable ventures. Immediately after the 1990 invasion of Kuwait by Iraq, he traveled to the Middle East to represent a large environmental company.

"I was fortunate to have the opportunity to facilitate contracts for recovery of the crude oil that had been discharged into the desert during the invasion," Bradford said. "I'll never forget seeing the tremendous lakes of oil in the desert and the hundreds of wells that had been set on fire."

Upon returning from the Middle East, Bradford got an opportunity to clean several hundred oil pits in the Amazon jungles of Ecuador.

"My experiences in Kuwait gave me the confidence and credibility to ask for and receive a decree from the president of Ecuador for the recovery and cleaning of hazardous oil ponds, which were polluting the drinking and bathing water of the people in the area," Bradford said. "This was perhaps the most satisfying project I've ever undertaken. I also participated in the building of schoolhouses and the donation of clothes and toys to children living in the jungle."

Bradford purchased Aimm Technologies, a specialty company that offers a patented cleaning process called Hydrokinetics, in 1995. The company serves a variety of industries — including petrochemical and food processing — and its process cleans tubulars in a manner that is quick and efficient and uses less water than conventional cleaning.

"In 1995, a longtime friend by the name of Ed Crook suggested I investigate the purchase of various patents for Hydrokinetic cleaning of tubulars," Bradford said. "Pat and Ralph Garcia, who owned Aimm Technologies, were attempting to assemble a company for the cleaning of exchangers and piping in the petrochemical industry. This was a perfect opportunity for me to return to my area of experience. After reviewing the attempted startup company, I decided to make an offer to purchase it. Ralph remained with the company and is still a friend of mine."

In its first two years, Aimm Technologies experienced negative annual profits. Undeterred, Bradford and his team trained crews, obtained equipment and structured a marketing plan that would eventually lead to profitability.

"Being known as a specialty company has been good and bad," Bradford said. "We've obtained 'almost-impossible' cleaning jobs and were successful, which gave us a lucrative position and a great reputation in our industry. The same success was also a liability in the early years because it prevented us from obtaining larger jobs and turnaround work. Many companies thought we were too small or too costly to perform routine maintenance. In the last four years, however, we have proved this to be wrong, and we are involved in several turnarounds annually. We have one sole-source contract with a major refining company providing total cleaning maintenance and vacuum truck services."

The company's domestic operations were expanded to places including Norfolk, Va., and Farmington, N.M., and two years after that, Aimm Technologies offices were opened in Thailand, Guatemala, Venezuela, Argentina and Brazil. Most recently, the company expanded to

"If you believe in what you're doing, don't ever quit. It doesn't mean that you can't alter some things every now and then, but you've got to stay on course."

Kenai, Alaska, where Aimm Technologies Vice President Lloyd Johnson — a 25-year veteran of the petrochemical industry — has worked to develop vacuum truck and cleaning operations.

"Our rapid expansion would not have been possible without an excellent team of employees and our patented cleaning process," Bradford said. "Although treacherous, working all over the world has been a success for our company. Each country in which we work has different rules, customs, religions and socioeconomic factors that determine success. We depend greatly on our local team of employees — Antone Belcher, Bo Davenport, Daryl Mickens, Robert Gill and Americo Almeida have thousands of Frequent Flyer miles from traveling to and from jobs that we've done. Our office manager, Linda Mettille, and Jamie Whittington — our contracts administrator and my personal assistant — have also been integral to our success."

Although he's experienced financial success and overcome a lot of obstacles, Bradford claims he is most proud of the way his son Brooks Jr. and daughter Heather — both Texas A&M University graduates — have moved into key positions within Aimm Technologies. Brooks Jr., a mechanical engineer, is the president of the company, and Heather, who has an accounting degree and is an expert in international tax and accounting, serves as vice president and chief financial officer and oversees the accounting department. (Brooklyn, Bradford's youngest child, is a junior attending Texas A&M.)

"They're taking it to a whole new level with their energy," Bradford said. "My son graduated from college on a Thursday afternoon, and by the following Saturday he was on a project in Chennai, India. They have a variety of broad experience between them, but I try to give them the benefit of my experience and keep them going down the middle of the road. They're entirely different from me and from one another, so that makes it a great relationship."

Bradford promised his children that he would give them at least five more years of service before considering retirement. But that was about five years ago, and he shows no signs of slowing down. The longer he stays on the job, the smoother the transition will be when he decides to step away.

"I don't think anyone has all the answers for a continuation of ownership within a family," Bradford said. "The advantages, however, far outweigh the disadvantages."

According to Bradford, he and his children are all strong-headed individuals who often have different ideas of how things should be done. More often than not, however, the differences in opinion result in mutually beneficial compromises.

"When two type-A personalities butt heads, it usually comes down to who has the hardest one," Bradford said. "But it's well worth it. I have a great deal of trust and confidence in what they do, and I'm learning from them. They bring segments into the operation that I would otherwise have had to contract out."

Heather, for instance, is a detail-oriented person who has a knack for preventing minor hitches from turning into catastrophes. Her experience with Fortune 500 companies and international tax prepared her very well for her current responsibilities.

"You should never let the pennies get in the way of the dollars, but it's important to look for little things that can create problems for you down the road if you don't correct them now," Bradford said. "A lot of that relates to the idea that your people are your strongest asset. We try to keep everyone challenged and recognize their accomplishments."

Bradford believes that self-starting, tenacious individuals can make any company successful as long as they are motivated and can maintain their focus.

"Whether you're looking for a technician, laborer, CPA or anyone else, you should hire the best people you can," Bradford said. "They should possess good business vision. For instance, we have technicians and supervisors who will go into plants and acquire additional work for us once they're in there. Your entire existence as an entrepreneur is based on the quality of the people you work with."

Bradford, center, is particularly proud of the way his children — Brooks Jr., left, and Heather — have moved into key positions at Aimm Technologies.

Of course, the mission of the people begins with the entrepreneur or manager, who must provide what Bradford referred to as the "sizzle on the steak."

"It takes a combination of things to be successful," Bradford said. "You must have a lot of drive, and you've got to be creative. If you have something that's special, that gives you a leg up on people."

Perhaps more than anything, an entrepreneur must stand ready to adapt to changing business environments and markets, and to face down the challenges inherent to any venture.

"If you believe in what you're doing, don't ever quit," Bradford said. "It doesn't mean that you can't alter some things every now and then, but you've got to stay on course. When you do that, you reach what I call operational excellence. Once you achieve operational excellence, you are able to work on the things that bring you and your business to the next tier, such as customer relationships and financial management."

Now that his children and the rest of his team members have taken the responsibility of running Aimm Technologies on a day-to-day basis, Bradford has more time to spend with Sandy, his wife of 35 years, who has been at his side through all the peaks and valleys of his journey to success.

"As my vision for the company becomes ingrained in my family, the transition of moving away from daily activities becomes easier for me," Bradford said. "When our customer base sees family members and key managers that share the vision, they know they're in good hands."

Though his work load will decrease as time goes by, Bradford will always enjoy traveling to his company's international offices in places like South America and Asia, and providing vision for his team.

The thought of failing has not occurred to Brooks Bradford in his lifetime. With Aimm Technologies poised to maintain its prominence under the leadership of his own flesh and blood and the other members of the company's management team, it likely never will.

JOHN
EGLE
President & CEO
Hub City Industries/Turbine Stimulation
Technologies/Louisiana Marine Transportation

In the fall of 2005, oil industry entrepreneur and lifelong Louisiana native John Egle retreated to the island of St. Thomas, located in the Caribbean Sea. As part of a fractional ownership he has with Ritz-Carlton resorts, Egle is able to travel at least four weeks out of the year to different destinations, including West Palm Beach, Fla., and Aspen, Colo.

It was a great time to get away, as anyone in America — especially in the Gulf South — knows. Hurricane Katrina had just days before ripped through Southeast Louisiana and the Mississippi Gulf Coast, rendering New Orleans uninhabitable and wiping towns like Waveland, Miss., off the map.

Egle, who resides in Lafayette, La., was not personally impacted by the storm. Like everyone else, however, he knew the toll taken on the oil and gas industry would be significant.

One day during his St. Thomas vacation, he received a call from a friend in the industry regarding a business proposal.

"He told me that he had work cleaning up an oil spill, but in order to do it he needed to buy a houseboat to provide transportation and living quarters for the crew," Egle said. "And he said, 'John, we have the job, but we've got to buy the boat right now.'"

Egle considered the proposal and, after some deliberation, phoned his bank. The friend picked up a check from the bank, and purchased two houseboats. Thus, Louisiana Marine Transportation, the latest in a long line of business endeavors undertaken by Egle, was born.

Entering into this agreement effectively filled Egle's plate. He is the president and CEO of Hub City Industries, a company specializing in well production services such as acidizing, coiled tubing, gravel packing, wireline P&A and cementing, and Turbine Stimulation Technologies (TST), which is currently developing a frac pump that is expected to revolutionize the well service industry.

You'd think that such great day-to-day responsibilities would make any businessman shy away from new opportunities. But that's never been Egle's style. Over the course of his career, he has managed a radio station, co-developed a waste treatment technology that is now a standard in the oil industry, grown previously sluggish companies into successful ventures and been part owner in restaurants and a car dealership.

During one period in the late '90s, Egle's investment portfolio became as full as it had ever been.

"At that time I had ownership in about 14 different companies."

That number may be surprising to some. But with such an amazing run of good luck — Egle had been successful in four major business ventures up to that point — it's no wonder he was willing to roll the dice so many more times.

Egle has never been one to shy away from adventure. While in his 20s, he spent two months traveling through Europe on a motorcycle, stopping only when he was left with just enough money to get home. One year later, he did it again.

Although Egle does not recommend that anyone emulate the course of his life, it's hard not to be encouraged by his story, which begins in the small Southeast Louisiana town of Golden Meadow.

* * *

In the late '70s, Egle's father ran a small AM radio station that broadcast in the Lafourche and Terrebonne parish markets. Egle studied communications at the University of Southwestern Louisiana (now the University of Louisiana-Lafayette) to prepare for a career in the family business.

That happened sooner than he expected — his father's untimely death left him and his brother to manage the station.

34

"We worked hard and made a little money, but there's not much money to be made in that kind of market," Egle said. "We were doing really well compared to other stations in the state."

The eventual departure of his brother, who went on to run for and win the office of Lafourche Parish President, left Egle in charge. Under his leadership, the station won Small Market Radio Station of the Year in 1981.

The radio station was a success, but the financial returns were relatively small. Still, Egle was content to manage his father's business — until an opportunity presented itself in an industry with which he had little experience.

"My brother-in-law asked me to help him get oilfield work in the Grand Isle area," Egle said. "So I ended up getting him a job for Conoco cleaning out large tanks of oil sludge."

At that time, there were no regulations against dumping oilfield waste into large pits on land. When Egle's brother-in-law cleaned the sludge and delivered it to a commercial pit, the owner of the land charged Conoco $5 a barrel. Approximately 30,000 barrels of sludge were dumped, resulting in a $150,000 payday for the landowner.

When Egle heard about how much money was made on that dumping job, a light went on in his head.

"I would work all year to get a shoe store to spend $100 on advertising with me," Egle said. "Naturally, I wanted more."

His ambition outstripped his knowledge, but Egle was undeterred. He set an appointment to meet Fritz Spencer of the Louisiana Department of Conservation to learn how he could get into the waste removal industry.

"He told me that they were outlawing pits, but were also looking for a new technology to treat oilfield waste," he said.

Egle left that meeting with more questions than answers. Two weeks later, however, Spencer called Egle and told him about a book he had read titled *Land Treatment of Hazardous Waste*. It was written for the EPA by Texas A&M University professor K.W. Brown. Spencer recommended that Egle contact the professor, who owned a consulting firm at the time.

"K.W. Brown told me that for $12,000 he could design an appli-

35

cation that could land-treat oilfield waste, so I hired him," Egle said. "We then looked for land and went through the process of getting a permit for the technology, which was the first of its kind in the oilfield."

The new treatment system consisted of a levee built around a grade of soil where waste was dumped and mixed with water and gypsum. The water was then removed from the waste and pumped into saltwater wells. Once dried, the waste was treated with nutri-

John Egle, right, teamed up ents, causing microorganisms in the ground *with New Orleans businessman* to devour the waste at a high rate. (Each *Kenny McWilliams in the late '80s* waste treatment area was called a cell.) *to purchase T&T Disposal, the name of which was later changed* The idea was good, but the timing was *to Land Treatment Systems. The* even better. The new regulations had put *company was sold to Campbell* pressure on major oil producers to treat their *Wells in 1990. Egle is pictured here with Clint Pierson, a partner* waste. *in Land Treatment Systems.*

Although things would get better as time progressed, there were initial design flaws.

"We didn't have a water treatment system in it," Egle said. "We had gotten a lot of rain one year, and it flooded the cell. We couldn't dry the cell, and there was so much water in it that we couldn't pump it down the well quickly enough to keep up. We had to shut it down for a while. It hurt financially."

Egle and Brown were forced to get a discharge permit and find an additional partner before they could design and fund the water treatment system required to dry out the cell. Once the problem was solved, work poured in faster than the new company — known as Intracoastal Oilfield Fluids — could handle it.

"It wasn't a matter of finding the work," Egle said. "The challenge was to keep up with it and learn enough about the process as we went in order to make it work. There was only a certain amount of waste that you could put into one cell and treat at any given time, and treating it took about a year. I had no experience in it, so for me it was all trial and error."

36

Despite the steepness of the learning curve, Intracoastal Oilfield Fluids was a quick success. The company's first major job was an $80,000 waste treatment for an Exxon drilling rig. It was Egle's first real taste of entrepreneurial success. He sold the radio station in 1985 to a cable television company in order to devote all of his time and energy to Intracoastal Oilfield Fluids.

"It would have taken us about six months to make $80,000 at the radio station," Egle said. "I was in my 20s and just out of college. To have a bill that big in such a short amount of time built my confidence."

Egle's involvement with Intracoastal Oilfield Fluids came to an end

John Egle learned the hard way that success is never a given.

in 1987, when his partnership broke down. He sold his share of the company to his partner, and immediately began looking for the next challenge.

T&T Disposal, a competitor of Intracoastal Oilfield Fluids, had recently built a five-acre land farm as a result of the Department of Natural Resources' regulation outlawing pits. When it came up for sale, Egle teamed up with New Orleans businessman Kenny McWilliams to purchase it. Renamed Land Treatment Systems, the company grew at an exponential rate. Two years later, McWilliams sold his share of the company to B.I. Moody and Tom Becnel, who funded additional expansion. In 1990, Land Treatment Systems was sold to Campbell Wells, a new division of Sanifill.

Egle worked for Campbell Wells until 1993, when he teamed up with six other investors to start Tri-Tech Fishing Services, a downhole oilfield service company. He and his partners expanded Tri-Tech over a three-year period and sold it to Smith International in 1997.

* * *

Like many entrepreneurs, Egle soon learned the hard way that success is never a given, even when you feel like the world is at your feet.

"Once we sold Tri-Tech in 1997, I'd had four successful companies in a row," Egle said. "So at that point I just started to invest in everyone."

Egle's interests included a Copeland's restaurant, a disposal company and a car dealership, among others. He knew even less about those businesses than the oilfield, and he devoted less time to overseeing their operations.

"I had quite a few things that didn't work at that time," he said. "That's when I learned I wasn't bulletproof."

Instead of panicking, Egle carefully weighed his options and cut his losses. Fortunately, he was able to change course before the situation could become unmanageable. He vowed to apply the hands-on approach that worked so well for him in the Intracoastal Oilfield Fluids days to all future endeavors. He also learned as much as he could about finance and committed to partnering with detail-oriented people who complemented his big-picture mentality.

During his time at Tri-Tech, an opportunity arose to invest in Hub City Industries, which was very small at the time. The company lay dormant under its initial management structure, but by 2000, Egle had begun the process of building Hub City to be the success it is today.

Having learned the virtues of prudence when investing in new ventures, Egle is more confident than he's ever been. Recently, he began a partnership with Ted McIntyre, president of Marine Turbine Technologies, and Chad Touchet and Glenn Dauterive of Hub City Industries to design and market a turbine-driven frac pump to companies drilling in shale in Fort Worth, Texas. The project was the brainchild of McIntyre, who has designed turbines for high performance watercraft, military vehicles and many other vessels, and Touchet, who origi-

From left, Ted McIntyre, Egle, Chad Touchet and Glenn Dauterive of Turbine Stimulation Technologies launched the JetFrac in 2006. Egle believes it is important to trust talented, hardworking and knowledgeable people in all business endeavors.

nally went to work for Hub City Industries in order to expand its fracturing business. The turbine-driven frac pump is expected to deliver numerous advantages, including a smaller footprint, increased hydraulic horsepower and the elimination of environmental hazards such as oil spills from diesel engines.

When Touchet and McIntyre first approached him about investing in the technology, Egle saw its potential almost immediately.

"It just looked like a better mousetrap," Egle said. "In an area like the Barnett Shale, they're drilling horizontally, and they're able to put up to nine stages in one well to produce from nine zones. Fracing is making that possible."

Egle enlisted the help of Dauterive, a longtime partner whom he describes as a "workaholic," to develop business within TST's target markets. The four partners expect big things for TST in 2007 and beyond.

* * *

Trusting talented, hard-working and knowledgeable people — and making them partners rather than employees — has allowed Egle to thrive as a leader and a visionary. It's the formula that first made him successful, and he's confident it will ensure stability throughout this new phase in his career.

A father of three, Egle hopes to decrease his workload over the next 10 years. Most of his time away from work has been spent raising his two daughters (ages 16 and 23) and his 17-year-old son. As the children grow older and their interests diversify, however, being a father requires more flexibility.

"My son plays hockey," Egle said. "I'll probably make about 10 trips to Dallas, Houston and Austin this winter to watch him play."

Egle would also like to squeeze in the occasional Aspen skiing trip or golf outing in the Virgin Islands whenever possible. Which begs the question — with such a full schedule, how many more times can Egle afford to answer the call to entrepreneurship?

"I'm trying to stop," he said, smiling.

HELEN I.
HODGES
President
Separation Systems Consultants, Inc. (SSCI)

What's more difficult: to start a business from scratch, or to purchase a fledgling company?

Many people, when asked this question, would likely say it is the former. After all, building a business from the ground up requires the energy, perseverance and imagination necessary to obtain capital and secure a customer base. But as Helen I. Hodges, president of Separation Systems Consultants Inc. (SSCI), will tell you, purchasing a relatively new business comes with its own set of challenges.

Hodges' résumé is something to be envied. After obtaining a bachelor of arts degree in physical science at San Jose State University, Hodges went on to earn Presidential Honors at the University of Idaho, where she received a master of science in chemistry. Later, she was transferred to Chicago, where she spent weekends and Fridays completing the University of Chicago's Executive MBA program and graduated as Valedictorian. She has worked for Argonne National Laboratory's Breeder Reactor Program, invested in and sold real estate, served stints as an international consultant and corporate strategic planner, raised and sold farm animals, and consulted small businesses. Her list of certifications and licenses in the environmental industry is a mile long.

When she and her husband Donald purchased the Houston-based SSCI from retired oil industry engineer Ed Wells in 1989, the company's primary focus was on nonhazardous oilfield waste pit closures in Louisiana. Hodges, who had lived in California, Illinois and Idaho for most of her life, had little experience in the Southeastern United States.

41

She learned quickly the difficulty in exploring uncharted waters, no matter how great the talents or impressive the qualifications of the explorer may be.

"The big challenge was coming here without having any real connections in the area," Hodges said. "We were dependent on the former owner and the existing customer base."

SSCI's established contingent of customers had made the deal more attractive to Hodges. A key apprehension, however, was whether loyalty would remain after Wells' departure.

"As it turns out, Ed was sensitive to the transition," Hodges said. "He did not want the company to fail, so he helped us."

With the help of Ed Wells and his wife Betty, Hodges and the SSCI team worked hard to maintain existing business and seek out new opportunities while dealing with the types of personnel issues inherent in any major transition. Some employees felt slighted by the sale, and others tried unsuccessfully to leave and take business away from the company. The true professionals in the firm, however, like A.E. (Whip) Baudin of Louisiana, embraced Ed's decision to retire and took pride in helping the company break all records in revenue and types of work performed.

Filling the shoes of Wells proved to be a daunting task for the new owner.

"Ed worked for Amoco previously," Hodges said. "Because of his strong character, he would be sent around the

Within two years of Helen Hodges' purchase of SSCI, the firm's earnings doubled.

world into problem spots, where he would work with odds-and-ends people who did not necessarily work as teams. But he was skilled at turning near-chaotic situations into effective, smooth-working operations. Following up a guy like that was tough because pulling the SSCI team together took a lot of management skill. Some personnel resisted moving in the right direction. I did not have Ed's skill level, experience or patience. Luckily, I had personnel experience from working at Argonne and as a small business consultant. So, at least my instincts were correct."

Years passed before Hodges had established a satisfactory level of comfort. But despite the challenges, the new-look SSCI was a great success. In just two years, the firm's earnings doubled. This was not an easy task considering that the end of the pit closure business in Louisiana forced the company to identify new markets for environmental services such as the evaluation, design, removal and installation of underground storage tanks (USTs); remediation; and services related to property transfers. But over the years, Hodges would build a diverse and talented team suited to taking advantage of further opportunities in consulting, management, training and permitting on a national scale.

* * *

When SSCI celebrated its 20th anniversary in 2006, the firm boasted a full suite of environmental and consulting services, along with an exemplary work record. The company has won major environmental engineering, assessment and remediation contracts with the Texas Department of Transportation (TxDOT) and a nationwide environmental site assessment contract with the Small Business Administration (SBA), among other achievements. Hodges has been honored by several professional organizations, including the National Association of Women Business Owners, the American Society for Training and Development, Who's Who in U.S. Executives, the Federation of Houston Professional Women and the Women Council of Realtors, among others.

For Hodges, building SSCI into a thriving, comprehensive environmental service company was never a question of "if" but "how."

"I tend not to wonder if something is going to be successful," Hodges said. "It's not a question of success or failure, it's more of a discovery of what works. Everything has 'doesn't works' to it. Management's job is to adjust actions to move along the continuum of results from the less effective and 'doesn't work' side of the curve to the effective and 'Wow!' ranges. That's the way I view things."

The course of her life has prepared Hodges for entrepreneurship. Born Helen Ambrosini, she grew up on a dairy farm in Northern California owned by her family. With her father, she managed and sold livestock, and her mother taught her business accounting. Both parents passed along superior interpersonal skills, the importance of staying true to her word and a commitment to giving back to the community.

Before she earned her degrees in the fields that would prepare her for work in the environmental industry, Hodges learned bottom-line orientation, coordination of assets and liabilities, and other product-line analysis basics. By 15, Helen had amassed a rabbit meat production and sales operation (nearly 100 rabbits at a time), raised and showed dairy cows and Herefords, and had already secured bank loans and lines of credit at feed and hardware stores.

"The technical part of a business, in my opinion, is the easy part," Hodges said. "The hard part is making sure you know what your company is doing. What is your company producing? How much money is it making? Where are you spending your money? Who in your organization are your key producers? It's just like owning a ranch. If you don't know which of those cows is routinely and efficiently producing calves for you to take to market, you're going to go out of business."

Later on in life, Hodges oversaw a cost-recovery program for Argonne National Laboratory in Idaho, which she described as something of a crash course in sales, marketing and personnel management. One of her department's responsibilities was to encourage Argonne scientists and managers to use in-house services like technical writing, photography and word processing.

"The important thing was to justify why use of an in-company department was a better deal than procuring the service outside at what seemed to be a lower price," Hodges said. "I learned a lot about sales. The diverse group within the cost centers I managed presented a number of personnel issues as well."

The diversity of her experience helped her to keep SSCI on stable ground in the early days. Even past agricultural experience was a plus, as SSCI moved into bioremediation and earth-moving projects.

"To me, the broader your experience base, the better," Hodges said. "At first I needed the technical expertise because I had to do some of the work. Now that we are the size that we are, I no longer have the time to spend on technical work, but it's good that I have the expertise because I can better understand problems that arise."

Her broad knowledge of the business has allowed Hodges to stay in tune with the needs of SSCI's customers, creating a personal touch that strengthens relationships over the long term.

"The company is still very much a mom-and-pop, in the sense that if our clients have technical problems, they can come directly to me and other senior managers," Hodges said. "I'm not going to solve their technical problems for them, but I can at least understand the issues."

Although nothing seems out of reach for SSCI, Hodges is happy to keep the company in the $5M range. She feels that further expansion would take away many of the little things that she enjoys the most about

> *"You must push hard on what you think is right. Then you stand back and take a look at what happened, set another path if needed, and push hard on that."*

running her business.

"Entrepreneurs come in lots of flavors," Hodges said. "Some want small businesses just to keep themselves busy. Others have a larger vision. Then there are people like myself who want mid-sized companies, and resist the temptation to become very large. I wanted a company that was big enough to have broad capabilities and well organized systems and procedures, plus a capable staff, but I did not want to be a key technical person. At our company, I have the opportunity to manage, but my vision is not to be a national conglomerate."

SSCI's size also allows Hodges and the SSCI team to quickly adapt to change and stay keenly focused on what makes the company successful.

"The small business owner really has to be technically based," Hodges said. "Our size means that I need some experience with all aspects of the business. As business parameters and markets change, I may have to re-involve myself with an aspect of which I am usually on the perimeter. Being a mid-sized business puts a burden that is different than if you are building a business with the idea of large-scale expansion. If you are planning large-scale expansion, you are after venture capital money and departmentalization of the company's processes or products. Building a large business requires a different set of skills than those needed by the small and mid-sized business owners. The guys that want to be big do not need a technical background — they can buy the technical knowledge needed and go for it."

While her ambition does not match that of the world's richest entrepreneurs, Hodges certainly shares with them the will to succeed and the determination to achieve no matter the odds.

"You must push hard on what you think is right," Hodges said. "Then you stand back and take a look at what happened, set another path if needed, and push hard on that."

Of course, the journey of an entrepreneur requires more than just persistence, resiliency and the ability to adapt to change. A skilled team of hard-working people who fit important niches within a company and understand the manager's ways of thinking and operating is essential.

"There's no question that you must have *your* team," Hodges said. "I'm not saying you need people who just support you. Actually, diverse ways of viewing the world and approaching projects are essential. A strong firm has a variety of people to assure all of the holes are filled. A monoculture in terms of the kinds of people at a firm is not healthy."

Over the past two decades, Hodges has seen many great people come and go. The company, however, maintains an energizing mix of new hires, multiyear experts and long-time veterans, such as Baudin, who has been with the company since before the purchase; Vice President Doug Jackson, another 15-year-plus technical wizard; David Klebieko, a 10-year-plus ecological expert; petroleum-system guru Paul Weaver; and accounting aficionado Susan Brown.

"As all good managers know, turnover issues can be neutralized when a company stays committed to consistency in the business model and a respect for employees," Hodges said. "SSCI is a fun and successful player because of the dedication, ethics, curiosity and 'can-do' attitude of its managers.

"A system is an extreme asset," she continued. "You have to create systems within the company that are reproducible, thereby eliminating time spent rediscovering methods and reinventing ways to do non-critical functions. Establishing that knowledge base is hard in a small company. But with a system, staff is not wasting resources or reinventing the wheel on simple things that have no relevance to getting more work."

* * *

With a strong team committed to delivering results in an expedient and efficient manner, SSCI is poised to build upon the success it experienced in its first 20 years. Although she still spends long hours at the office, Helen is now able to focus considerable energy on other passions, including ranching, community service and spending time with her husband Donald, a real estate and development entrepreneur in his own right, and sons William (Bill) and Donald, both of whom are in college. The

The Hodges family owns a ranch in Santa Fe, Texas, on which they raise reining horses and livestock for beef production. From left are Helen, her husband Donald, and their sons William and Donald.

family owns a ranch in Santa Fe, Texas, on which they raise reining horses and livestock for beef production.

Hodges and SSCI are key supporters of the Armand Bayou Nature Center, a 2,500 acre nature preserve located in Houston's Bay Area region, and the company has been involved with the reefing of the Texas Clipper, which will become an oasis for marine life and a destination for divers on the Texas coast. The Hodges are also working to create a 600-acre preserve on the coast of Northern California near Helen's childhood home of Ferndale. Hodges serves on other nonprofit boards, most notably the Center for Women's Business Research located in Washington, D.C.

Of all the reasons Hodges can give for her personal success, whether it's timely and economical management of environmental projects, perseverance, people skills, determination, luck or anything else, none has been more instrumental than the belief that she's a winner. This

47

was instilled by her parents back in the days when work was as simple as milking a cow.

"From early on, my family instilled a 'you are successful' view," Hodges said. "It was always either that I was the 'A' student or I should have been. My mother would say, 'You're going to be President someday.' My dad always gave me big responsibilities. If a child is made to believe he or she is a winner, the subconscious creates successful behaviors."

A less healthy perspective would likely have led to misfortune early in her career with SSCI. But Hodges has a way — a system, if you will — of moving from one vantage point to another without losing confidence or energy.

"When bad things happen, you must try something different," Hodges said. "To my way of thinking, any kind of upset is simply an odd thing. With that point of view, you are curious as to why something did not work, which causes you to take a moment to figure out and adjust to what does better. To me that's a really important way to view life."

JON
HODGES
CEO
Evergreen Industrial Services

When Jon and Jackie Hodges informed their personal CPA of their intent to purchase the struggling industrial services company Waterpoint in 2000, the accountant forecast two rather bleak outcomes.

"He said we'd either be flipping hamburgers or asking people if they want to Super-Size," Jon Hodges said.

Hodges first went to work for Waterpoint on the advice of trusted friend and business mentor Malcolm Waddell.

"Malcolm had been working with Waterpoint as a consultant," Hodges said. "One of the things he told them was if they wanted to grow, they needed to hire certain people to get them there. He gave them my name."

Hodges already had a great reputation for being a troubleshooter and for developing business. After a brief career in the maritime industry, Hodges went to work for BFI Chemical (Enclean) in 1984 — just three-and-a-half years before it was purchased by Main Tech, a full service company owned by Waddell and Tim Tarillion. Main Tech later merged with a chemical cleaning company called Park Chem and became known as Enclean. While at Enclean, Hodges was responsible for growing a new environmental services division in Deer Park, Texas. He brought the initial revenues from $1.4 million to $7 million in just two years. He later opened another yard in Texas City, Texas, with revenues beginning at less than $500,000, and grew it into a $10 million operation.

Hodges had officially begun his career as the go-to person for floundering locations. Shortly afterward, he was asked by an Enclean regional manager to take on the management of the company's Freeport, Texas, facility, which was losing approximately $600,000 per year. Under Hodges' leadership, the branch soon became the fourth most profitable facility in the company.

Brand purchased Enclean and another company called Naylor, which was based in Freeport and Texas City. After that deal was completed, both Naylor facilities and the Brand yard in Victoria, Texas, were merged into Hodges' operation. He brought both Naylor facilities from the break-even point to profitability and was then promoted to regional manager of Southeast Texas and put in charge of Brand's mega-yard in Baytown, Texas. (He describes this as being given the keys to a Cadillac.) The Baytown mega-yard was ranked first in profitability out of 52 divisions during the two years Hodges managed it. His other facilities also ranked in the top 10 — Texas City was second, Freeport was fifth and Victoria was seventh.

In 1994, Brand was purchased by Rust, a corporation that owned Waste Management, Wheelabrator and several other companies. Though it was a tough decision, Hodges elected to leave his job of 14 years in order to join Waterpoint, which offered equity.

"I had everything you could ever want available to me at Rust," Hodges said. "But Malcolm Waddell said to me, 'Jon, I think this is a good chance for you.' So I took the deal."

Hodges hit the ground running at Waterpoint, opening branches for the company in Sulphur, La., and Beaumont and Port Arthur, Texas. In three years, Waterpoint's revenues increased fivefold. The honeymoon didn't last, however. Waterpoint's finances were badly mismanaged, and the company was soon left swimming in debt.

"I actually worked out a deal for HydroChem to purchase Waterpoint for $15 million," Hodges said. "It would have been a good thing, but the majority owners elected not to sell at that time. I just remember being so disappointed. They would have managed the company a lot better."

Approximately five months after HydroChem's letter of intent to purchase was declined, Waterpoint declared bankruptcy. Rather than look for a different job, Hodges considered purchasing the company himself in order to rebuild its foundation and bring it back to profitability.

"Waterpoint had a lot of secured creditors," Hodges said. "The bankruptcy trustee sold the creditors on going forward with me instead of closing the company and moving on. It was a five-year deal, but we cleared all the debt with the secured creditors, including the bankruptcy trustee, in one year. It's really a success story."

* * *

The La Porte-based Evergreen offers a full spate of services, including tank cleaning, waste minimization, hydroblasting, vacuum services and more, to the refining, chemical, petrochemical, power and paper industries in the Gulf South and beyond. It took a monumental effort and considerable time to rebuild the company from the ashes of Waterpoint, but not an eternity. Hodges chalks the relatively quick success up to smart management.

"I've seen people do really good things in this business, and I've seen people do some really stupid things," Hodges said, laughing. "I've always tried to not do the stupid thing in any given situation. It's a rule of thumb that's helped me a lot."

Hodges believes the problems of Waterpoint brought the best out of him and the Evergreen team.

"Anybody can run a business that's doing well," Hodges said. "Unfortunately, these types of businesses go through cycles where they don't do well. I think that is where I excel the most. When a business isn't doing well, I'm the kind of manager you love to have on board."

The mental toughness to face down challenges is vital. The maintenance of the resulting success, however, requires an equal amount of strength.

"Company structures and personalities change when revenues increase," Hodges said. "Our revenues are at $25 million right now, and our goal is to keep it under $50 million because I'd like to stay focused on the

Jon Hodges, right, visits with friend and colleague Walter Treybig of Sterling Chemicals.

51

business. Once you get over that $50 million hump, you have a tendency to be less visible."

Invisibility is a natural by-product of ballooning success. But that's not the Jon Hodges way of doing business. He and his management team have created a system that ensures routine interaction with clients.

"I like to know who all my customers are," Hodges said. "I really enjoy getting out and meeting with them on a regular basis. I think it's been paramount to our success."

His ability to maintain strong personal relationships has also enabled Hodges to build the best team in an industry in which people tend to bounce from one company to another. In the earliest days of Evergreen, he had a list of people he wanted to hire, some of whom he couldn't afford to bring on board right away. Once the company was able to generate the required amount of revenue, he was able to begin assembling his "dream team" of environmental service veterans, including Rick Pitman, director of safety and training; Craig Byard, national tank cleaning manager; Bill Stephens, tank cleaning sales manager; and others.

"We've got people on board who have been through acquisitions and have been with companies that burst through the $20 million mark," Hodges said. "They've all made this tour, so it's nothing new to them. They understand that in a changing environment, there is still more to do and a different set of things that come to you. This staff is well-versed in those situations."

Hiring people he knew made Hodges feel confident that Evergreen would exceed its objectives. Under Pitman's guidance, Evergreen has logged nearly 2 million man hours without an OSHA recordable incident. Byard has spurred major growth in the tank cleaning division, and Stephens has developed a top-notch marketing program.

Of course, no manager can build a team entirely out of experienced veterans if he hopes to achieve the level of success experienced by Evergreen. In cases where a manager must lead untested team members, patience and imagination are necessary.

"One thing that's helped me is the ability to move people," Hodges said. "I think everyone is good at something. I've always been able to take people who aren't doing well in one position, make them feel confident in their skills and put them in another position more geared toward their talents. Eventually we find where they need to be."

All of Evergreen's key employees have some level of ownership within the company. Like all good managers, Hodges knows that instilling a sense of ownership goes a long way in motivating an individual to give you his best, day in and day out. That's true even when the boss reminds his partners each day that no matter how successful the company is, there is always room for growth and refinement.

"I do tend to focus on a lot of the negatives," Hodges said. "The things that are running smoothly don't need to be fixed. I know the posi-

"My father was very disciplined, and he never liked to hear me say that I couldn't do something. So from a young age I learned that it's better to start solving issues than to make the excuse that it can't be done."

tives are there, and I feel good about them. But when we meet, we're there to talk about areas in which we can improve. I don't know if that's a positive or negative thing."

So far it's been a positive. Hodges has overseen the growth of three companies since he first decided to travel down the path of entrepreneurship. Shortly after he purchased Evergreen, Hodges also founded Industrial Pump & Supply — a safety equipment and pump supply company — and H&H Properties, which owns both industrial properties and condominiums.

In 2002, Hodges formed a partnership with Kim DeYoung and Fred Pyle and formed TIBC. TIBC sells, leases, rents and services container boxes (i.e. filter boxes, roll-off boxes, vacuum boxes) to the refining and petrochemical industries. Hodges, along with his partners, started TIBC as an enhancement to the industrial cleaning division. Little did they know at the time that TIBC would grow to the $10.5 million operation it is today.

No man responsible for such lucrative enterprises can be successful without staying keenly focused on what can go wrong. Given the things he witnessed in the days before founding Evergreen, Hodges should know that better than anyone.

* * *

At the age of 45, Hodges still finds himself spending 14 to 16 hours per day at the office. He also finds that the peaks and valleys of a day's work are not forgotten when he returns home in the evening.

"A lot of my brainstorming seems to happen right when I should be going to bed," Hodges ruefully acknowledged. "I find myself lying down and thinking over situations that I don't feel good about for two to three

Hodges' wife Jackie, who holds a degree in finance, was instrumental to the founding of Industrial Pump & Supply.

hours. When I go into the office the next morning, it's time to meet and go over the things I 'slept' on overnight."

The team that has worked for Evergreen in its six years of existence deserves tremendous credit for the company's success. But Hodges never ends a conversation about what he's achieved without mentioning those closest to him.

Hodges said he is fortunate that Jackie, whom he declares to be "the best wife in the world," understands the challenges of entrepreneurship. A graduate of the University of Houston's finance program, she was instrumental to the founding of Industrial Pump & Supply and oversees its day-to-day operations. While she has no official responsibilities in the operation of Evergreen, her constant moral support of its chief executive is a thankless job. In their precious leisure time, they enjoy boating — particularly in Destin, Fla., and on Galveston Bay in Texas — and collecting vintage sports cars and motorcycles. They have three children — a son who is involved in the day-to-day operations of TIBC and is learning the intricacies of management, a daughter who is a student at the University of Houston, and another daughter who attends Clear Creek High School, the same school where her parents and siblings graduated.

Hodges' mother, a longtime civil servant, is credited with instilling in him a knack for understanding people and their individual needs.

"My mother is a very generous person," Hodges said. "She communicates very well with others and tries to build a team concept with everyone she works with."

Hodges also points to the memory of his father, a 30-year veteran of the Army, as a heavy influence, particularly on the way he approaches problems.

"My father was very disciplined," Hodges said. "He never liked to hear me say that I couldn't do something. So from a young age I learned that it's better to start solving issues than to make the excuse that it can't be done."

To Hodges, there is no such word as "can't," even on those days when he's paying the price of a long night spent ruminating instead of resting.

"I can sit in a meeting all day long and nearly fall asleep, but when somebody says, 'Well, we just can't do that,' my eyes pop open," Hodges said. "When someone says that something can't be done, I feel beholden to challenge them on it."

Hodges proved from the beginning of his life as an entrepreneur that nearly anything is possible. In 1999, he set a three-pronged goal for his new venture — to secure sole-source agreements with Exxon Mobil in Beaumont and Huntsman Chemical and Sterling Chemicals in Texas City. All three objectives were met within one year. The feat is quite remarkable considering that the other companies bidding for the work were significantly larger than Hodges' fledgling operation. But Hodges, a man with super-sized expectations, would have settled for nothing less.

"It was a just a matter of staying on top of the situation, knowing the people, setting the strategies and moving forward," Hodges said.

KEITH
HUBER
President & CEO
Keith Huber Inc.

The spirit of invention has pervaded the American consciousness since before our nation was born. It seems as though with each new decade, a different crop of new and exciting products, systems or processes is making our lives more convenient or enjoyable.

Where does this spirit come from? Are inventors born with it? Is it acquired through prodding and experience?

Most would probably say it's a little of both. A majority of those who can be fairly characterized as inventors possess a rare combination of intelligence and quirkiness. Some can even be described as eccentric.

Few, however, possess not only inventiveness, but also the business sense and the dogged determination of an entrepreneur. In that number is Keith Huber, founder of Keith Huber Inc., the nation's leading independent manufacturer of mobile vacuum loading equipment.

Raised on a farm in rural Illinois, Huber developed at a very early age the work ethic that would propel him to success in his adult years.

"Hard work was never in question," Huber said. "It was just something you did every day of the week."

From the time he was six years old, Huber carried a heavy work load — he was responsible for milking cows and feeding livestock. As he got a little older, he began building fences, maintaining farm equipment and tearing down barns one nail at a time in order to reuse the materials.

Within every child is a vivid imagination. Since Huber spent considerably more time working than most boys his age, it's no surprise that many of his ideas involved the creation or enhancement of farm equipment.

Keith Huber's first true innovation was a flag holder made for farm tractors.

"With little time to play, I found enjoyment putting my visions to work," Huber said. "I was always fixing or modifying the Allis Chalmers equipment my dad used on the farm. Every so often, an Allis Chalmers field representative would visit our farm and observe my modifications. They eventually incorporated some of those modifications into their future models."

Huber continued to invent gadgets for the farm as he grew into his teens.

"The one I remember most was a post puller I made when I was 18 to jack steel posts out of the ground," Huber said. "We used it for many years, and we still have it to this day."

His first true innovation, however, was a flag holder made for farm tractors. A law was passed in those days that required tractors to carry red flags 12 feet above the ground. This caused headaches for farmers who could not pull their tractors into sheds due to the flags being so high in the air. Huber designed a spring-loaded fixture that allowed flags to be folded down, and sold several hundred to local farmers.

"At the age of 19, I worked for T Birdie Corp., which manufactured golf carts," Huber said. "They were impressed by my design ability and soon had me doing custom products. The following year, they called me in to build a snowmobile for them in an effort to offset their summer product."

Not long after he was assigned the task of building the snowmobile, the T Birdie factory closed. Nonetheless, Huber went to work in his 20-foot-by-20-foot shop and finished the project. He showcased the finished product at the Second World Snowmobile Round-up at Yellowstone National Park, to high acclaim.

"The manager I had worked for got a group of investors together to produce the machine, which they called the Chaparral," Huber said. "It became the No. 1 selling snowmobile for a couple of years, but I received nothing but an 'Atta boy!'."

Huber then went to work designing another snowmobile, which he showcased at the Minnesota State Fair. The vehicle was a big hit, and he sold 40 units on the spot. Lacking a facility in which to produce the snowmobiles in bulk, however, he sold the design, fixtures and sales to Mallard Coach of West Bend, Wis.

"With the money from the snowmobile sales, I constructed a new building, bought the inventory from the old golf cart company and began producing golf carts under the name FLAGMASTER," Huber said. "I began with three-wheeled carts and later started building a four-wheeled cart with a patented suspension. Some of those are still running today, and are coveted for their magnificent ride."

Huber also designed a modular electric personnel carrier called the X-pediter that was later used to transport the Rockettes at Radio City Music Hall in New York City.

In his early 20s, Huber built a snowmobile and showcased it at the Second World Snowmobile Round-up at Yellowstone National Park, to high acclaim.

It was at this time that Huber began to find out that the life of an entrepreneur can be as smooth as a ride on a wooden rollercoaster. Cheap imports made it impossible for U.S. manufacturers to compete, and the three major golf cart companies ceased manufacturing golf carts. Despite the popularity of the X-pediter, the profit margin was thin, and Huber soon found himself out of money.

"All of a sudden, I was contacted by a huge conglomerate in the Northeast," Huber said. "One of the principals of the company had ridden in one of my golf carts and thought it was the best ride in the world."

The company offered to purchase FLAGMASTER, but Huber had already given up on the prospect of ever turning a profit.

"I told the principal that it was pretty much over and that I was broke," Huber said. "He encouraged me to hang on, but I didn't. Shortly after I closed the doors to the manufacturing company and auctioned off the equipment, I received a check from him by mail, but it was too late. I had missed the boat."

After receiving the check he could not cash, Huber recalled stories of people who, in his words, had stopped digging for gold just short of the mine. He vowed to persevere when and if the next opportunity came along, no matter how challenging it would be. But before that, he was faced with the task of overcoming his own feeling of failure. For a man who had worked hard every day of his life, being unsuccessful for even a short period of time was truly disheartening.

* * *

Huber returned to his hometown in the early '70s and went to work for IME, a division of Pearson Brothers that manufactured vacuum trucks.

"I had known Lee Pearson my whole life," Huber said. "He let me share his space at the Minnesota State Fair the first time I showed my snowmobile."

Over the next few years, Huber traveled all over the United States selling vacuum trucks. Though he enjoyed sales, Huber's heart was always in design. He convinced Pearson to allow him to show the IME staff a new way to manufacture trucks. The method, which used SAE standards from truck body builders' books, allowed each module to be built individually and bolted to trucks.

"The design allowed for many combinations of options," Huber said. "It was a new concept at the time, but it is now used by almost every manufacturer in industry."

Although he left IME in 1978, Huber's gift of innovation would once again open doors for future endeavors. He began to receive phone calls from other manufacturers inquiring about his design concept. Huber founded his own company — Keith Huber Inc. — in 1982. With only a small amount of money to invest, he constructed a 40-foot-by-60-foot building in Gulfport, Miss., and spent the next 15 years working harder than he ever had before.

"I recognized that suppliers of raw material and parts would play a big role in trying to start a business with little money," Huber said. "The first step was to call each of them and try to get their products with terms of net 30 days. This meant the supplier would give me the materials with no money up front. When the material came in, however, there was just 30 days to build the vacuum system, mount it on the truck chassis and deliver the new unit to the customer."

For Huber, working at such a feverish pace made days and nights blend into one another. He recalls very little from that 15-year period beyond working and the occasional breakfast at Waffle House. But he did what was necessary to build his fledgling business from the ground up, and in 1998, Huber cut the ribbon on a 54,000-square-foot facility expan-

"If you stay focused and never give up in the face of adversity, things will work out."

sion. It brought the total size of his plant to 118,000 square feet — quite impressive considering what he had to start with.

At the ribbon cutting ceremony, Brian Giglione — an employee of Keith Huber Inc. at the time — introduced Huber thus:

"The technology and products we produce as a company, the environmental harmony we achieve, the vision for the future that we see is empowered to us by a creative, understanding, relentless individual. I truly believe that this individual realizes his largest accomplishments when he witnesses the growth of someone else."

By that time, Keith Huber Inc. was successful enough to support a payroll of 130 people. Huber owned several million dollars worth of real estate and had enough money saved up to build his dream home.

"Things couldn't have been better," Huber said. "I was 56 years old and felt that my lifetime of hard work and dedication had really paid off."

More hard times, however, were just around the corner.

* * *

In 2001, sales at Keith Huber Inc. began to fall. The downturn of the American economy had been exacerbated by the terrorist attacks of Sept. 11. Huber had experienced challenges before, but had never fallen from such great heights as he achieved in the late '90s.

"I was concerned, but I'd been through downturns before, and they had never lasted long," Huber said. "Even though we didn't have enough orders to support our work force, I hesitated to lay anyone off. It is very hard to find good people, and I had the best. I knew that if I could just hold on long enough, the economy would pick back up and things would get better."

The economy, however, did not improve for another three years. Huber was forced to carry out what was, without a doubt, the hardest task he'd ever faced up to that point — lay off employees. It was an emotionally trying time for Huber, but he and his remaining staff soldiered on.

As business began to pick up in the last quarter of 2004, Huber received a patent for an air inverting cyclone for the company's largest vacuum system, the AIRLORD®. In December, Keith Huber Inc. received an order for 128 AIRLORD units from an Iraqi company contracted by the United States government to help rebuild the country in the wake of the 2003 war that toppled the regime of Saddam Hussein.

"Finally, I saw light at the end of the tunnel," Huber said. "But experience had taught me to hold excitement close to my chest. There were still a lot of details to work out."

Among the details was the financing of the materials needed to build the AIRLORD units. (Keith Huber Inc. would not receive payment for the units until 30 days after they arrived in Iraq, which would take at least 40 days by boat.) Many of the financial institutions Huber approached balked due to the instability in Iraq.

"That was the first blow," Huber said. "But we had a contract to honor, and the first unit had to be shipped by July 1."

The company was able to meet the deadline, but there was still no financing plan in place. Then, an unexpected turn of events threw the whole deal into a tailspin.

"Although we had received an order for 128 units, the government funded only 33," Huber said. "We had to contact our suppliers and tell them to cut the order, but some had already sent their materials. There was no turning back."

Keith Huber Inc. took a big hit as a result of the reduced order, but was able to recover over the next several months.

"Production was going smoothly," Huber said. "I felt really good about the progress and was sharing how good things were with a friend one day when he said, 'Well, we sure don't need that hurricane that's out there.'"

The hurricane Huber's friend referred to was none other than Katrina. What would turn out to be the most devastating natural disaster in U.S. history was creeping toward the Gulf Coast. So consumed was Huber with maintaining the strength of his company that he'd gone weeks without watching television or reading a newspaper.

"We had already been forced to evacuate twice that year due to hurricanes that ended up turning elsewhere," Huber said. "I hoped it was just another false alarm."

Huber went to bed at 3 a.m. on the morning of Aug. 29 after securing everything he could. He woke up the next day to violent winds that sounded as though they could shake his home to its foundation.

"I mentally assessed all the bracing we had added to the house when we remodeled it seven years earlier," Huber said. "When the hurricane passed, I had only lost a couple of windows, a fence and some trees."

Relieved, Huber traveled to his facility. On the way there, he noticed that many of the homes in Gulfport had not been spared the destruction his own house had eluded. He began to worry again.

The Keith Huber Inc. facilities in Gulfport, Miss., were heavily damaged by Hurricane Katrina, but by late 2006 the company had recruited more than 100 new employees and sales were increasing.

"When I arrived at the plant, I found that all five buildings had been ripped apart," Huber said. "The facility looked like it had been bombed."

Huber walked among the debris that was strewn around his

118,000-square-foot facility with a familiar feeling. Adversity had presented itself in many different forms over the course of his career, but never on such a scale. Large portions of the facility he had worked 23 years to build lay in ruins. Many of his employees were rendered homeless. Rain was still falling as the storm rolled to the north.

Perhaps if he hadn't already experienced the crushing sense of defeat that ensues when a man gives up on a dream, Huber would have packed it in. Instead, he remembered the vow he made to himself all those years ago when he shut down his first manufacturing company and missed the chance to benefit from its promise.

With the help of a few employees, Huber began to clean up the grounds of the facility and move the company's equipment out of the rain. Dave Flagg, a pump supplier and friend of Huber's, brought food, supplies and a group of volunteers who worked to patch a hole in the Keith Huber Inc. fabrication building and cover its offices with tarps.

"Three months later, we were ready to resume production in a limited facility," Huber said. "Only 35 of our 97 employees returned to work. Some had decided to go into business for themselves cleaning land, repairing roofs or building homes. We also lost some of the remaining 35 to FEMA, which was offering huge pay for moving and hooking up temporary trailers for evacuees."

Huber and his reduced staff also began contacting customers to explain the situation and inform them of the company's new delivery schedule.

At the time of this writing, Keith Huber Inc. had recruited more than 100 new employees, and sales were increasing. Huber has also acquired 70 acres of industrial ground that is being subdivided for rental space, which is being taken by suppliers of Keith Huber Inc.

Although he is well aware that each new day brings with it the prospect of adversity, Huber knows now more than ever that a challenge is just another opportunity to create success out of a bare minimum of resources. Any man who possesses the gift of innovation knows that's true, but experiencing it several times over only serves to strengthen his resolve, which he finds to be a necessity when the storms of life come roaring into the atmosphere.

"If you stay focused and never give up in the face of adversity, things will work out," Huber said as he reflected on the challenges of his long and ultimately successful career. "It's been 61 years of hard work, vision, dedication, determination, learning, sacrifice and faith. A lack of any one of these would have resulted in a different path."

Huber is keenly aware that although he's overcome many obstacles to achieve the stability he now enjoys, one can never be sure about what lies ahead. But the relentlessness referred to in Giglione's 1998 introduction doesn't allow him to do anything but work harder until the challenges of today become the rewards of tomorrow.

A man of less mettle may view a life of constant challenge as a nightmare, but Huber simply refers to it as "the path of an entrepreneur."

"Life is full of plateaus," Huber said. "We must always stand ready to climb to the next."

DAVE
JOHNSON
President & CEO
Sparkling Clear Industries

It isn't always easy to find your way in business, especially if you enter a field that's quite different from one in which you've gained years of experience. Houston entrepreneur Dave Johnson, who purchased Sparkling Clear Water Care (now Sparkling Clear Industries) in 1985, can attest to that. Having spent the majority of his career in industrial sales, Johnson knew nothing about the residential water filtration systems marketed by Sparkling Clear Water Care, much less the sale of those products.

"I was president of an electronics company that was purchased by a holding company based in Australia at the time," Johnson said. "The holding company was doing a rollup into another company here in the United States. I had recommended the deal to the owner and told him he couldn't afford not to take it."

Shortly after the deal went through, however, Johnson decided that he'd prefer to strike out on his own than to work for a large, public company.

"I could see that my philosophy didn't fit their type of operation," Johnson said. "During my time with the old company, I had brokers looking out in various cities for different businesses for sale that might fit into our operation."

One of those companies was Sparkling Clear Water Care, which had intrigued Johnson before but was not a good fit for his previous employer.

"Even though I didn't know anything about the business, I had come to the conclusion that it made more sense for me to go out on my own than to have no control over my own destiny," Johnson said. "My two kids were finishing college, and I just said, heck, it's time for me to do my own thing."

Shortly after purchasing Sparkling Clear Water Care, Johnson purchased another company based in Clute, Texas, that had a small filtration contract with Dow Chemical.

"My background had always been industrial, so that was the direction in which we wanted to go," Johnson said.

Johnson entered the residential water filtration business with nothing but a talent for selling and a never-say-die attitude. Due to economic circumstances, however, it was difficult for the first-time entrepreneur to make a splash in the market.

"The more we got into it, the more we realized that the timing was probably not the best," Johnson said. "Houston was in the process of entering its first recession, and interest rates were going through the roof, so we had little core business residentially."

Johnson persisted, deciding that even if no money could be made in residential water filtration, there had to be a need within industry that his company could fulfill.

"When my son got out of college, he went to work at our Clute office and found that there was a need for a service-minded bottled water company in the plants," Johnson said. "So we entered the bottled water business, and that was our first move into the industrial world."

Johnson and his company came up with innovative ways to deliver water to the plants, and the business grew. Soon enough, however, the 20-percent rate of interest on the loans being taken out by the company became burdensome.

"We couldn't keep borrowing money, or we were going to go broke very quickly," Johnson said. "There's no way to make a markup to absorb that kind of thing if you're not operating on cash flow. So we had to find some ways to generate money on a short-term basis. The big challenge was finding someone to sell to so that we could keep the cash register ringing."

Inspiration came to Johnson one day during a lunch outing at Brady's Landing, a restaurant that offers its patrons a view of the Houston

Ship Channel.

"I'd watch the ships go by and look at all the smokestacks," Johnson said. "Then, I'd drive back and forth across the Loop 610 bridge and see plants as far as the eye could see. And I'd say to myself, 'They've got to be buying something else that I can sell to them.'"

Dave Johnson sands down rust on a used truck purchased during his days in the bottled water business. Sparkling Clear Industries evolved a number of times before its current incarnation as an industrial filtration company.

It was then that Johnson decided to explore the market for liquid and air filtration products used by industry. He went into information gathering mode, sifting through resources to find product manufacturers and visiting buyers in industry and heavy manufacturing to inquire about the competition.

"I spent an awful lot of time in the filtration section of the *Thomas Register*," Johnson said. "I used that as a springboard for talking to different manufacturers about their products. As we began to accumulate contacts in the filter world, we then began to identify the top five or six filtration people in the area and asked their customers what they liked and didn't like about them."

The data gathered from the research allowed Johnson to develop a business plan that would distinguish his company from its competitors. He also discovered in the course of the fact-finding mission that the companies he targeted were experiencing widespread demographic shifts among their personnel due to the recession.

"They were retiring people early to cut costs and replacing them with people who didn't have the experience or the knowledge of where to buy filtration products," Johnson said. "So we decided to become a resource for that, even though we didn't really have any product lines. We began an extensive cross-reference list of all types of filtration and related products. If they didn't know where to buy it, they could call us, and we'd find it for them."

Johnson sold the residential filtration business and continued to deliver bottled water to plants to raise cash flow as the company expanded into industrial filtration. The name was changed to Sparkling Clear

69

Industries, and the team spent the next decade working hard to secure its identity and build strong relationships with vendors.

* * *

Johnson's life as an entrepreneur has been beset by obstacles. The economic pressures of the '80s and the challenge of making it in an unfamiliar business ensured that the road to success would be rocky, to say the least. On top of all that, Johnson experienced some of a businessman's worst nightmares, including disputes with the IRS and the horror of seeing one of his residential filtration sales representatives on the 10 o'clock news after the man had been arrested for kidnapping a child.

"There were times when it seemed as though we were moving like a snake — sometimes forward, and sometimes sideways," Johnson said. "We had more downs than ups in the early days, but since it was my decision to do the thing, I was obligated to put the best spin on it that I could. If I'm walking around feeling like I'm down in the dumps, my guys are going to say, 'What the heck am I doing here? I'd better go out and get a job, this thing's going down the tubes!'"

If Johnson seems uncharacteristically positive, it's because he inherited that mindset from his father, a landman who contracted tuberculosis in 1943 and was forced to conduct all of his business from a sanitarium located in the family's hometown of Shreveport, La.

"There was no cure in those days," Johnson said of his father's disease. "Communication was difficult, but he had to keep some semblance of business, even in the isolation of that sanitarium. There wasn't a phone that he could use, so he had to write everything down on paper and give it to my mother. She would then make all of his phone calls at our house and report back to him."

Fortunately for Johnson's father, penicillin had been developed to treat casualties of World War II and was becoming available on the homefront at the time of his illness.

"He ended up surviving, even though he was left with half a lung," Johnson said. "Through it all, he continued to work and never complained. He had a goal, and that was to take care of his family, which he did."

Johnson also attributes his winning attitude to his participation in sports during high school and college. (He played football and baseball and lettered in swimming at Southern Methodist University.)

"If you play sports, you have to keep a positive attitude and stay focused," Johnson said. "You never go into a venture to lose. To me, failure is never an option."

Often times the fear of failure can lead to creative solutions to problems. Johnson experienced this on one occasion, during a particularly lean period, when a plant called to request a piece of carbon dioxide filtration equipment with which he was unfamiliar.

"When you're struggling, people don't call to ask for the things

"You never go into a venture to lose. To me, failure is never an option."

you have in your inventory," Johnson said. "They only call you for the things they can't find. But we needed the business, and so we had to figure out where to find what they needed and how to put it together for them."

Johnson and his colleagues were able to deliver, and the job paid enough to keep the company afloat for at least another month. That episode still stands out in Johnson's mind as an example of how an entrepreneur can overcome an adverse situation by taking time to think of the best solution rather than fretting over his misfortune.

"If you're going to be an entrepreneur, you must have the mental dexterity to create activity until you can get the ship righted," he said.

Righting the ship is a team effort, according to Johnson, who has learned the hard way that even the most well-rounded manager can only extend himself so far.

"I've always had a talent for revving up sales, so that's what I like to do," Johnson said. "As long as I stick to that, I do pretty well. When I try to run something, I generally foul it up. But that's part of what makes a team — you have one guy pushing the engine and another guy polishing it. Generally, if you're a budding entrepreneur, you don't have a large staff. So if you can generate sales but can't manage what you've sold, that's a problem."

Johnson didn't set out alone. Ed Wasser, with whom he worked at the previous company, came along with him to manage the company's operations. Johnson readily admits, however, to having been more hands-on than he should as his company evolved.

"Because we changed direction three different times — from residential filtration to bottled water to industrial filtration — I didn't pull the trigger on some of my duties quickly enough," Johnson said. "I kept my nose in the operational side, which is not my strong suit.

"I'm a pot stirrer, but there's only so much a business can stand, and at some point the pot needs to simmer."

Now that Sparkling Clear Industries has established its product lines, it maintains a steady base of vendors and clients. The pot has simmered, leaving Johnson and his wife Annette a little more time to spend with their two children and their families, and raise longhorn cows on their ranch.

"Anyone who's going into business and has a family should think twice about becoming an entrepreneur if they're not willing to put their spouses and children first," Johnson said. "I know many entrepreneurs who have worked hard to succeed in business, only to lose their families. I am very grateful to my wife and kids for having stood by me all these years, even during the hard times."

Those who expect success to come easily can't be faulted for their optimism. It's happened to many people, but such good fortune is rare. More often than not, budding entrepreneurs learn quickly that the business world is a battlefield, and that those who lack the courage and the resources to fight will not win in the

Johnson and his wife Annette enjoy spending time with their two children and their families, and raising longhorn cows on their ranch in Texas.

end. But if they do possess the courage to fight valiantly for their survival, chances are they will become stronger, more creative and more satisfied when they finally succeed.

"I see many people who have tremendous talent and wonderful ideas, but they're not prepared for the onslaught of problems that occur when they don't have business coming in every day," Johnson said. "In most cases, you don't. If you're going into business, you can't prepare for the rewards — you have to be prepared for the problems. And if you can't handle the problems, then you shouldn't have done it in the first place."

Johnson's ability to persevere has allowed him to remain positive through his latest personal challenge — in 2005, he was diagnosed with prostate cancer. Since the diagnosis, he has become involved in Us TOO International — a support group founded by prostate cancer survivors — and he hopes to someday publish a resource book designed to help men deal with the emotional element of the disease and encourage them to seek as much information as possible before undergoing medical treatment.

DAVID
LACOOK
President & CEO
FabEnCo Inc.

On the day he turned 32, FabEnCo President & CEO David LaCook had a choice — either celebrate with his family and friends or drive from his home in Houston to New Orleans to demonstrate his company's patented Safety Gate to a Union Carbide plant in Taft, La., the following morning.

At the time, FabEnCo was still being run by its co-founders — David's father, Hardy LaCook, and Don Henderson. Motivated by his desire to bring new business to FabEnCo, David put his birthday festivities on hold and hit the road.

"Union Carbide had run across the Safety Gate in the *Best Safety Directory* and were considering using it at the Taft plant," David said. "They wanted to replace all their chains with the gates, and so they requested that someone come over and do a demonstration."

The decision turned out to the be the right one. After observing the capabilities of the Safety Gate, Union Carbide ordered 400 units, giving David something to boast about upon returning to work.

"It was a tremendous order for us at that time, and it was the first big one that I could really hang my hat on," David said.

Being the son of the boss no doubt helped David gain a foothold at FabEnCo, but his father didn't make it much easier than he would have for anyone else. David's achievement was just the latest in a series of milestones that set the stage for him to succeed his father as president and CEO when Hardy retired.

"In the summer of 1972, I was your typical teenager, sleeping

75

until noon and so forth," David said. "Finally, my mother told my father to get me out of the house, so he put me to work. In those days, he was getting to the office at 4:30 or 5 o'clock in the morning, so I quickly got into the habit of trying to get an early start and being productive."

Hardy enlisted his son's help with bookkeeping and cost accounting, a task David enjoyed almost immediately.

"In manufacturing, it's vitally important to know what your component costs are because they greatly affect profits," David said. "I found I had a real aptitude for crunching numbers, so I changed my high school curriculum to bookkeeping."

After graduating from high school, David enrolled at the University of Houston and studied business administration for about a year-and-a-half. He soon found, however, that college was not his cup of tea and went to work full time building vessels as a shop employee for FabEnCo.

According to David, working in the shop was considerably less cozy than crunching numbers. He spent long days putting 45-degree bevels on shells with a grinder. The work was intensive, but it gave David the chance to prove to his father's managers that he could handle even the toughest jobs.

"If you worked all week doing that, picked up your paycheck, and

came back to work on Monday, the shop foreman knew you wanted the job," David said. "After about six months in the shop, I went back into office administration, and I've been there ever since."

David is living proof that a real-world education can get you just as far as one received at a university. At about the same time that David took his career-making trip to Louisiana, the Houston area was in the throes of a crippling recession.

"We had been trying to get

Invented in the '70s and offering fall protection at ladder, platform, mezzanine and stair openings, FabEnCo's Safety Gate was an ingenious product with the potential to sell in high volume in industry. David LaCook recognized this in the late '80s, at what would prove to be the turning point in the history of the company. (Photo: Houston Chronicle) into the energy equipment business for about four or five years, but that bottomed out," David said. "We had a shake-up — the chosen successor to my father's leadership at that time left the company."

David stepped into the vacuum of leadership at a time in which the future of FabEnCo was uncertain. With the company in debt and experiencing low revenues, David became its vice president and took on the responsibility of helping to figure out the way forward.

Hardy had invented the Safety Gate in the '70s, but he never dreamed that it might someday be his company's bread and butter. Offering fall protection at ladder, platform, mezzanine and stair openings, the Safety Gate was an ingenious product with the potential to sell in high volume in industry. David recognized this at what would prove to be the turning point in the history of FabEnCo.

"Every time we spent a little money promoting the Safety Gate, our revenues seemed to go up," David said. "We didn't have to service it after it was sold, and it made good money for us. We put a routine focus on promoting it, and it just took off like a rocket."

A decade later, FabEnCo had fully redefined itself as "The Safety Gate Company." In 1993, Hardy retired from the company, putting David in charge of a FabEnCo that, while very different from the one founded in the '60s, was on course for tremendous growth in the years to come.

Don Henderson, left, and Hardy LaCook celebrate Hardy's retirement from FabEnCo in 1993. Hardy and Don were the company's co-founders.

* * *

Ever since being named an executive at FabEnCo, David has spent considerable time studying books on management. Not long ago, a financial advisor suggested that David listen to a book on tape by Michael E. Gerber titled *The E-Myth Revisited* that discussed a common trap that ensnares many budding entrepreneurs.

"Gerber says that the entrepreneurial trap is when a guy finds something he really likes to do in life and starts a business, but eventually goes nuts because he's being dragged away from what he likes to do by other things, like taxes and insurance," David said.

According to Gerber, in order for a business to be successful, the management team must consist of a visionary (someone who understands the industry and can make inferences about its future), a technician (someone who understands operations and logistics) and a business manager (someone who understands the administrative needs of the company).

"Many businesses fail because they don't have those three disciplines," David said. "It's very difficult to find them all in one person."

FabEnCo was fortunate enough to have a visionary, a business manager and a technician during the late '80s and early '90s. Hardy was the visionary, David blossomed into a business manager, and Don, a long-time veteran of the fabrication industry whom David often referred to as his "second dad," was the technician. As the careers of Hardy and Don winded down, David began to participate in The Executive Committee (TEC), a worldwide association that allowed business managers to share best practices with one another. (TEC is now referred to as Vistage.)

"My interest in TEC came from the recognition that the dads weren't going to be there forever," David said. "When I would come up with wild and crazy ideas, Dad and Don would say, 'Well, this is what happened when we tried that.' So we were always able to filter ideas to deal with current issues through their experiences and modify them for successful implementation."

Knowing that he wouldn't always have the luxury of filtering ideas through Hardy and Don, David began to think about how he might fill the void.

"I learned during the course of leadership development that a real leader doesn't have the answers to everything," David said. "His primary job is to ask questions and make sure that all his employees have the tools and resources to do what needs to be done. He should listen to his people because they are the ones who know how to run his business. I've never been a general. I like to think that I'm good at delegation, and I'm certainly interested in what other people think about different situations."

The lessons learned during the TEC meetings only enhanced the business acumen David gained coming up through the ranks of FabEnCo. During a period in the late '70s when the company experienced financial problems, David learned how to deal with accounts payable, which in turn aided his development as a communicator.

"One of the things I learned at that time was how to tell someone that although you can't pay them right away, you have a plan to do so in the near future," David said. "I've found that as long as you keep the lines of communication open with people, they'll work with you. I think some folks just don't know how to say 'We can't pay you,' but we learned how to do that and to work with people in those situations."

"The question we always ask ourselves is, 'Are we having fun yet?' No matter how dark the situation is, we try to find something to smile about. That keeps your mind in the right place to start finding a solution, whatever the challenge might be."

Two years after the financial slump, David made many payments that had long been written off by other companies.

"That probably caused more bookkeeping problems for them than if we hadn't paid at all," David joked. "But integrity is one of our values, and I don't think you can find anyone in the business world today who wouldn't say that FabEnCo pays its bills."

When the struggles of the '80s began to affect FabEnCo, David replaced a practice he refers to as "bank-balance management" with a budgetary approach that entailed definite and reviewable goals and prevented financial mishaps resulting from unsuccessful investments.

"Previously, we would take risks to grow the company, pursuing those ventures until we ran out of cash," David said. "Then, we'd stop and focus again on what we did best and try to recover. Now, we still take the risk, but the venture must meet certain objectives to receive continued funding. This protects our core business from being negatively impacted."

For FabEnCo, the recovery was tied to the quick success of the Safety Gate, making the management of cash flow relatively simple.

"When we reinvented the business, it gave us a chance to evaluate how we did everything both in our production facility and in the office," David said. "From a business planning standpoint, it was very simple — we knew what the payroll, the payroll taxes, the debt and loan payments and the accounts payable were going to be. So the plan was to sell enough gates to meet that cash flow every month and start digging ourselves out of the hole."

David's father had founded the business not only with his own money but also contributions from others. Financial assistance came from a number of friends, colleagues and family members, so at the time of the company's wholesale reinvention, many shareholders monitored the activities of FabEnCo closely to ensure the security of their investments. For David, the responsibility of protecting the interests of those outside the day-to-day operations provided further motivation to him and the FabEnCo team.

"One of the shareholders was a man who is still in the pipe-selling business," David said. "He once told us that we were broke and we just didn't want to admit it."

The resolve shown by the FabEnCo team as they returned to prosperity is among the very few things that could not be taught in any boardroom or classroom. It was the kind of perseverance shown only by people who truly believe that they will be successful no matter the odds. David rewarded the team members who remained loyal to the company during the lean years by instituting an employee stock ownership plan (ESOP) in 1990 that also helped ease the transition of ownership from generation to generation.

For David, the passion and commitment was personal. After all, FabEnCo was the family business, and it was his responsibility to become the "dad," so to speak, when the other father figures were ready to move on.

"My father used to tell me, my two brothers and my sister that there was a perception that job security involves working for a big company, and how that was proven not to be the case," David said. "He said that the only security you really have is working for yourself. That way there's only one person who's going to provide for you, and whether or not you make it is on your shoulders."

* * *

FabEnCo recently celebrated its 40th year in business, and is now as strong as its ever been. Sadly, Hardy and Don, who passed away in 2000 and 2001, respectively, were not able to see the company enter its fifth decade. They would no doubt be very proud, however, of the job David and his team have done.

David likes to tell the story of a small gift he gave his father when he left FabEnCo in 1993.

"My dad and Don used to have a saying — 'Old age and treachery will overcome youth and skill,'" David said. "When

FabEnCo is now led by President David LaCook, left, and Executive Vice President Don Henderson.

Dad retired, we gave him a plaque that said, 'Youth and skill overcame old age and treachery.'"

Humor has always been a key ingredient in the success of FabEnCo. At trade shows, the company employs an artist to sketch caricatures of booth visitors being prevented from falling off a platform by the Safety Gate. David prides himself on being able to view almost any situation in a positive light.

"The question we always ask ourselves is, 'Are we having fun yet?,'" David said. "No matter how dark the situation is, we try to find something to smile about. That keeps your mind in the right place to start finding a solution, whatever the challenge might be."

Sustaining a smile has always been easy for David, who loves his work and considers it a hobby in and of itself. After all these years, he is still an impulse traveler — in November 2005, he delivered three Safety Gates to a plant in Norco, La., that was preparing for an OSHA VPP inspection. The plant called at 9:30 on a Friday morning and asked that the gates be delivered by 5 p.m. Half an hour later, a member of FabEnCo's administrative personnel informed the plant representative that the president of the company was on his way to deliver the gates in person.

"To me there's nothing more enjoyable than traveling around the country and preaching the gospel of gates," David said. "It lets me see the countryside, meet lots of people and study a little history."

David claims to have had a keen interest in the American Civil War since age 12. As a matter of fact, his great-great grandfather participated in and survived Pickett's Charge at Gettysburg, which is considered to be the bloodiest single military attack in American history. David has tracked the history of his ancestor's family in the course of his travels and could probably write a novel with the information he's obtained.

When not on the road or at the office, David enjoys spending time with his wife Carol and his 14-year-old son Daniel, who recently discovered his talents for playing the piano and the French horn.

It wasn't a challenge for David to find his calling, though due to circumstances beyond his control, fulfilling his potential was no walk in the park. Still, David's story is encouraging to those who don't believe that the road to success begins at a university and nowhere else.

"We tell people too often that if you want a decent job, you need a college degree," David said. "But I know an awful lot of plumbers, electricians and carpenters who make great livings without degrees. My father taught me that the best place to find out what you want to do in life is to go to school. You'll find out there, even if you decide not to complete a degree program. If getting a college education is not what you want to do, you should study business. Whatever it is that you like to do, chances are you can run a business doing it.

"I believe the key to true happiness is to make a living doing something you really enjoy."

JOHN
MCNABB
Founder and Chairman
Growth Capital Partners, L.P.

As the founder and chairman of Growth Capital Partners, L.P. — a firm that provides investment and merchant banking advice to middle-market companies — John McNabb must stay in touch with the needs of business owners and work tirelessly to ensure that they are fulfilled. Fortunately, he had the opportunity at a young age to forge a strong work ethic in a labor intensive environment under the watch of his grandfather, a World War I veteran who owned one of West Virginia's largest meat-packing and processing firms until his death in 1957.

From the age of 10, McNabb worked summers at the plant performing a wide variety of small and large jobs. He began working in the plant's freezers, but as he grew, he began to haul and pack boxes of processed meat and eventually drove a delivery truck. His father, who also worked for the family business, was a skilled salesman who traveled to coal-producing towns in the family's home state of West Virginia to service accounts. McNabb would often ride along with his father, a habit that provided him with many great lessons about dealing with various personalities.

The combined influences of his father and grandfather had a profound impact on the young McNabb, who always took pride in the success they created and maintained for the family and for the company's employees.

"My grandfather only had a third-grade education," McNabb said. "But he was very smart. He was a voracious reader, so he was self-taught. And he was a great leader — his employees always had an image of him as being larger than life."

McNabb's grandfather expected that his grandson would someday run the business, but the family opted to sell it after his grandfather passed away. A gifted athlete, McNabb was offered a football scholarship at Duke University in 1962, and he went on to become the first member of his family to attend college.

As a multipurpose football player for Duke, McNabb was an integral part of one Atlantic Coast Conference (ACC) championship team and earned several personal accolades, such as being named most valuable player of the 1965 squad, winning the

A gifted athlete, John McNabb was offered a football scholarship by Duke University in 1962. While at Duke, he was named a captain by his teammates and won all-conference and All-America honors.

ACC's Jacobs Blocking Trophy and garnering All-America honors. During his senior year, he was named a captain by his teammates, a distinction he had earned several times before both in high school and youth league sports.

"In high school, I was a captain of the football, baseball and wrestling teams," McNabb said. "Those positions were always picked by the players. I never thought about it while I was growing up, but I guess I had an aura of leadership that came across to my peers. I'm really proud of that now.

"I remember during my senior football season at Duke that after four games, we were unbeaten and ranked 11th in the country," he continued. "We played Clemson at home with Orange Bowl scouts in attendance. We had six red zone turnovers, including a game ending fumble on the goal line after a long drive and lost, 3–2. Several key players got injured and we lost our next three games. We had Wake Forest and North Carolina left and before the Wake game, two other captains and I called a late night team meeting at a small cemetery on campus by the football stadium. The meeting was an open forum on togetherness, trust and winning. The next day, we beat Wake Forest 40-7 and then went on to beat North Carolina — who had beaten Ohio State in Columbus, Ohio, earlier in the season — 35-6 and won the ACC championship. I learned a lot from that team meeting experience. Listening and focus played a role in that leadership exercise."

Whatever leadership skills he didn't inherit from the men in his family he learned by observing his athletic mentors at Duke — Head Coach and College Football Hall of Famer Bill Murray and Athletic Director and Hall of Famer Eddie Cameron. (Cameron, who coached both basketball and football at Duke, is the namesake of the university's Cameron Indoor Stadium, where the men's and women's basketball teams play their home games.)

"Bill Murray was a great coach and an excellent leader," McNabb said. "He was a stern disciplinarian, but he was also a gentleman. We didn't see his gentle side during practice or in games, but we knew it was there. Eddie Cameron was also a great leader. He was the epitome of a gentleman."

Another person who influenced McNabb was Terry Sanford, the president of Duke University. Sanford had previously served as governor of North Carolina and as a United States Senator from North Carolina. (McNabb worked with Sanford at Duke while completing his MBA.)

"Terry and I met incredibly interesting people as I traveled with him for meetings with leaders such as Henry Ford Jr., John D. Rockefeller III and John DeButts of AT&T, just to name a few," McNabb said. "I watched Terry as he handled those meetings and their exchange of ideas. He was a politician, but also a World War II combat paratrooper and a great competitor. Observing those meetings was an education in and of itself. He taught me the value of listening and focusing on the ideas and perspectives of others."

After graduating from college, McNabb had an opportunity to play professional football. He could have easily signed on to a squad in the NFL or its Canadian counterpart, the CFL. It was 1966, the peak of what many consider to be the golden age of professional football. Legendary coaches like Vince Lombardi of the Green Bay Packers and Tom Landry of the Dallas Cowboys were still earning their places in history. Johnny Unitas, Gale Sayers and Joe Namath were young and on the cusp of greatness, and the first Super Bowl (then known as the AFL-NFL World

Championship) was still a year away.

The lure of professional football was strong for young athletes back then, just as it is today, but the compensation was mediocre at best. McNabb had spent the past four years of his life balancing the myriad responsibilities that come along with playing sports and getting a college education, and was exhausted. Having been the first in his family to attend college, McNabb decided that he'd prefer to make the most of his education and took a manufacturing supervisory position with DuPont in Richmond, Va.

Not long after that, however, he was drafted into the military and chose aviation. He served two combat aviation tours during the war in Vietnam — the first in 1969 and the second in 1971 — and earned the rank of captain. During his 15 months of active overseas duty, he participated in approximately 147 combat missions over Laos, North Vietnam and South Vietnam, and was nominated for the Pacific Air Force Junior Officer of the Year distinction during 1970. He was awarded several medals, including the Air Medal with three oak leaf clusters and the Distinguished Flying Cross.

After completing his military service, McNabb returned to Duke to pursue an MBA in finance. By the time he earned his master's degree and re-entered the work force, he was in his mid-30s.

* * *

McNabb went to work for Mobil Oil's exploration and production division in 1979, starting out in Denver and later transferring to Dallas. He left Mobil after about three years and later joined The Prudential Insurance Company of America, where he eventually would enjoy a successful stewardship of The Prudential's direct energy investments. He left The Prudential having built an investment portfolio of over $4 billion and in 1989 became managing director and board member of the Houston-based BT Southwest Inc., a wholly owned subsidiary of Bankers Trust New York Corp.

Although his career had been very successful and his leadership potential was fulfilled, McNabb began to feel a desire for independence

86

that had originated during his days with Mobil.

"It's not that I was critical of big companies," McNabb said. "I had learned a lot while working for large entities. But I wanted to make more of a difference, and I didn't think I could do it in that type of organization."

McNabb saw that there was a need for quality merchant banking assistance among companies in the Southwest valued in the $20 million-$200 million range and he began to formulate the idea for Growth Capital Partners. He teamed with David Sargent, a close friend with whom he'd worked during his first years at The Prudential, and Charlie Stephenson, a

"You don't see many acts of bravery in business. You do, however, see people standing up for what they believe in and taking the high road. You have to be able to do that in a new venture because you're going to be tested."

colleague who had successfully built and sold Andover Oil and who had started Vintage Petroleum, to found Growth Capital Partners in 1992.

"There were some really good people in the financial services business in the Southwest," McNabb said. "Our feeling, however, was that there was a void with respect to quality financial advisory assistance for smaller companies. Many of those private companies are owned by entrepreneurs, and those people often times had difficulty in finding competent assistance as it relates to capital markets expertise and selling their businesses. It may have been an outrageous overestimation of what we could do, but we decided that we would try to make a difference for entrepreneurs and smaller companies."

McNabb and Sargent, the two operating partners, founded the company in Houston and immediately began to help entrepreneurs and private company owners achieve personal and financial goals. Services included assistance with company sales, raising private equity, recapitalizations, management-led buyouts, workouts and restructurings, and debt financings.

Despite their belief that Growth Capital Partners would be a success, McNabb and Sargent had to overcome the challenge of operating in a region in which they were relatively unknown.

"Neither David nor I grew up in the Southwest, so we didn't have a lot of built-in friendships or contacts," McNabb said. "It helps to know people, so that made it difficult. It was very hard to get people to drink the Kool-Aid, so to speak. They'd ask, 'What is Growth Capital Partners? Who are you and what have you done?'"

Once McNabb and Sargent secured their first clients and yielded great results for them, they were able to start building greater name recognition for Growth Capital Partners within the industry.

"As we've grown the business over time, we've tried our best to be responsive to people who refer business to us," McNabb said. "We have relationships with a half dozen great law firms in the Southwest, and they send us business from time to time. We have also been blessed to have some terrific relationships with larger full-service investment banks that send business our way. A big source of deals for us comes from entrepreneurs and business owners whom we have assisted in the past. That's been a huge help because when you start out with just a few people, you don't have enough time to do an effective job of marketing your services."

Meanwhile, the company maintained a keen focus on market trends and database management, started to build a significant transaction track record, and began to attract a diverse crop of talented and experienced people who bought into McNabb's and Sargent's vision.

McNabb, right, teamed with David Sargent, left, and Charlie Stephenson to found Growth Capital Partners in 1992. McNabb and Sargent are the firm's managing partners.

"We've been able to attract some really top-flight people who have stayed with us through the years," McNabb said. "They bring a lot to the table in terms of relationships and deal making. Some have had experience in

88

running businesses, and that's been a huge help to us. We're not just a bunch of bankers. A fair percentage of the people in our firm have direct operating experience, have served on boards or have been private investors themselves."

The combined experience and expertise of the Growth Capital Partners team has allowed it to thrive in the 15 years since its inception. It serves clients in the energy, manufacturing and distribution, retail, and technology industries throughout the Southwest, New England and Western Canada from offices in Houston, Dallas, Austin and Greenwich, Conn. Growth Capital Partners has helped many industrial service companies sell to other entities, including Anco Industries, which was purchased by XServ Inc.; United Industrial Services, which was sold to Ohmstede, Ltd.; and MGM Well Service, which was purchased by Integrated Production Services Inc.

Growth Capital Partners also is in the direct investment business through its mezzanine lending arm — Southwest Mezzanine Investments (SMI). SMI manages approximately $100 million. Fund 1 has had realizations on all of its investments and yielded a gross return in excess of 20 percent.

"We have tried with Growth Capital Partners to address market needs through SMI Funds 1 and 2," McNabb said. "Starting our fund practice is another form of corporate leadership that has been beneficial both to our marketplace and to our firm."

* * *

While serving in Vietnam, McNabb witnessed many acts of bravery. Although the acts of bravery committed by soldiers and civilians in wartime are quite different from acts of bravery committed by strong-willed entrepreneurs, the mindset is essentially the same. McNabb draws the distinction by defining the actions of people in the business world as courageous rather than brave.

"You don't see many acts of bravery in business," McNabb said. "You do, however, see people standing up for what they believe in and taking the high road. You have to be able to do that in a new venture because you're going to be tested."

Besides courage, McNabb believes that an entrepreneur operating in a vacuum must remain committed to his primary objective in order to succeed.

"Focus is incredibly important because when you're out on your own, there's no feedback and no analogies," McNabb said. "Often times entrepreneurs put themselves in a position of second-guessing themselves. The only thing you can do to get around that is focus on your plan but be willing to change if the results aren't what you expected. A great example of that has been demonstrated by my brother, Bob McNabb, who runs a worldwide human capital business for Korn Ferry International. Bob's focus and drive to achieve have been inspirational to me."

Since the world of today is vastly more connected than it was just a few decades ago, constant change is an important fact in the business world. Businesses and markets evolve faster than ever, and those who refuse to change with the times often find themselves lagging behind in their respective industries. McNabb often refers to a quote by Tom Peters, author of the book *In Search of Excellence* and brother-in-law of David Sargent, to illustrate the importance of adaptability.

"One summer I was talking to Tom and David about a book I had read," McNabb said. "That book discussed how the past way of thinking was, if it's not broken, don't fix it. Tom's theory, however, was just the opposite. He said if it's not broken, break it. With the information flow of today, everyone is more aware of each other's business, so you have to constantly refine your business to maintain competitiveness. You also have to continue to improve your own knowledge base, which leads to both professional and personal improvement."

McNabb is also a strong believer in the importance of humility and service, especially when dealing with stakeholders in a public company.

"Today public company directors have a huge fiduciary responsibility to their shareholders," McNabb said. "This is an awesome responsibility that cannot be taken lightly. I have served on six public company boards. Professionalism in the board room has grown exponentially."

The virtue of teamwork carried McNabb to success on the football field and the battlefield. When he struck out on his own as an entrepreneur, the same concept held true — working together for the benefit of everyone involved puts the team on the path to victory. McNabb and Sargent kept that in mind as they built Growth Capital Partners.

"The main thing we look for is integrity," McNabb said. "Occasionally you'll hire someone who is great, but doesn't fit into your culture. But by and large the people who stay at Growth Capital Partners have great integrity, and because of that, we're a very open place. I've been in places that are closed and very political, with people spending more time backbiting than creating value for the company or in the market. We don't have that here because we let people know in the hiring process what our culture is all about. And so the integrity, the team orientation and the communication skills of our people become our culture because that's what we look for. It's one and the same."

In his spare time, McNabb enjoys spending time with his wife, traveling, reading, listening to music and piloting his Bonanza A-36 airplane. McNabb has a son who runs a successful supply-chain management consulting firm in Melbourne, Australia, and a daughter — a former investment banker — who lives in Asheville, N.C., with her husband, who runs a successful hedge fund. McNabb also has a stepdaughter who is a professional in the human capital industry in Houston and a stepson who is a high school lacrosse player.

As his business continues to grow, McNabb remains faithful in the power of people, both inside and outside the business world.

"I have a lot of great friends, and I spend a lot of time talking to them," McNabb said. "Whether or not it's related to business, the interaction is just great for me. Some of our friends have been investors in my firm, which helped us a lot in the beginning. Their willingness to say that we were worth buying into meant the world to us."

RAYMOND L. "BUBBA"
NELSON JR.

Founder and Former Chairman & CEO, Allwaste Inc.
Principal Founder, Sanifill

No one wants to take a pay cut. Especially when it's to the tune of about 75 percent.

In the early '70s, Louisiana native Raymond L. "Bubba" Nelson was sitting pretty in the waste industry. The McNeese State University graduate held an important post with Browning-Ferris Industries (BFI), which had just a few years earlier bought his family's solid waste and landfill business. As a division vice president for acquisitions, operations and market development, by 1977 Nelson was drawing an annual salary of approximately $80,000.

The next year, he worked harder than he ever had in his life — sometimes spending 10 hours on the road per day and doing jobs that required days instead of hours — but would only make $20,000.

Such is the life of a budding entrepreneur.

Nelson had left BFI to found Allwaste Services of Texas in 1978 after witnessing the success of a colleague in the industrial waste removal business. With only a single air mover mounted on a truck chassis, Nelson put his dream of building a company into first gear and never looked back. He traveled to industrial sites all over the Gulf Coast and worked tirelessly, cleaning smokestacks, tanks and blast furnaces. For the first two years, Allwaste was a one-man company surviving on gumption alone.

Less than a decade after its inception, Allwaste went public and was ranked second among *Forbes* magazine's 200 best small companies just two years after that.

Now retired, Nelson reflects on his career with the gleeful satisfaction of a Hall of Fame quarterback who's won two or three Super Bowls, though he is quick to credit the people who made his success possible along the way.

Not surprisingly, Nelson was a gifted athlete in his youth — he lettered in three different sports as a student of Sulphur High School in Sulphur, La. He was always the first to arrive at the baseball diamond, the gridiron, the basketball court, the golf course and the track field and the last to leave.

With only a single air mover mounted on a truck chassis, Bubba Nelson put his dream of building a company into first gear and never looked back. In its first two years, Allwaste Inc. was a one-man company surviving on gumption alone.

"I can remember going home well after dark because I was so enthused about the different sports I played," Nelson said. "I carried that on into the business. It's exciting to accomplish something, no matter how tired you are."

There are few things tougher for a human being to ignore than his own physical and mental exhaustion. But as Nelson proved during the early days of Allwaste, a good night's rest is just one of the many sacrifices any industrial service provider has to make in order to be successful without anyone's help.

"On one job, I strung up 100 feet of 12-inch steel pipe and cleaned out an incinerator," Nelson said. "I worked for 72 straight hours. If they'd stopped me working for five minutes, they never would have been able to wake me up."

Once Nelson was able to hire some employees, a healthy sleep pattern was reintroduced, but he didn't rest on his laurels. Through hard work, hands-on customer service, benevolent management and sound strategy, Nelson and his team built Allwaste into a major player in industrial services.

* * *

The Allwaste business model was fairly simple. Once the company was up and running, Nelson and his management team began to approach potential investors based in areas in which they wanted to gain a foothold. When an investor bought in, he was given 80 percent of the company's holdings, and the Allwaste team would essentially run the day-to-day operations of a new branch in the investor's home region. A line of credit was given to the investor for four trucks. The investor was then given stock in the company, and the startup was rolled up into Allwaste the day it went public.

"All of the investors were people I knew pretty well," Nelson said. "I propositioned them and they jumped at the chance. Some of the guys who supported our startups became millionaires."

The investors required that Nelson go public with Allwaste at $5 per share. If that didn't happen, they were given the option to divest. In 1986, Allwaste purchased Guzzler Manufacturing, a Birmingham, Ala.-based vacuum machine manufacturer, and the combined assets of the two companies allowed for a public offering that elicited high demand.

"We were fortunate enough to be six times oversubscribed," Nelson said.

After the public offering, Allwaste continued to expand through acquisition. It purchased Independent Tank Cleaning Services of Atlanta the following year, and The Bassichis Co., a Cleveland-based glass recycler, in 1989, along with a number of other family-owned waste companies.

By the time Allwaste was sold to Philip Services of Toronto in 1997, the company had completed 160 acquisitions and employed more than 4,000 people. Its industrial and environmental services included on-site industrial cleaning and waste management, waste transportation and processing, wastewater pretreatment, site remediation, container cleaning, maintenance and repairs, and emergency spill response services. Its annual revenues were greater than $400 million. Nelson was also the visionary and a founder of Sanifill, a sanitary landfill company based in Houston that was purchased by Waste Management in 1996.

That's an impressive track record for a man who began his career driving garbage trucks. Although life has been good to Nelson, success has not spoiled him. If you were to travel back through the years and the

95

millions of dollars and meet the young Bubba Nelson who hauled solid waste for Nelson Industrial Services, you'd likely see the same hardworking fellow with a smile just as wide as the one he carries nowadays.

* * *

Nelson claims to have enjoyed every moment of his career, from the early days in the family business to his retirement from Allwaste.

"I can't say I ever had a bad minute at Allwaste," Nelson said. "From the first moment I started the company, I knew it would be a success. I never looked back."

Ironically enough, as a youth he aspired to take a different course in life.

"I would love to have been an attorney, but my grades weren't good enough," Nelson said. "Although a lot of entrepreneurs don't have formal education, you don't have to teach them how to work hard. But when a guy like myself builds his own company, he has to work hard and work smart."

Fearing he'd never make that transition, Nelson found people who possessed the skills needed to carry out jobs that were outside his areas of expertise.

"They did the smart things, and I kept the company under control," Nelson said. "I was the glad-hander. I'd go out into the field and talk to the people because that was my forte. I wasn't an accountant or a lawyer or anything like that, so I left those things to other people. I am strictly a people person."

A large part of what's kept him humble over the years is the satisfaction he's taken from helping other people to grow and fulfill their own dreams.

"I love seeing people improve their lives," Nelson said. "I got the biggest kicks out of watching people in our company elevate themselves. Those are the moments I'll never forget."

Nelson related as an example the story of a young man in Mobile, Ala., who worked as a hydroblaster. Earl Bryant, who ran Guzzler Manufacturing, recommended that Nelson consider the man for the top management position at Allwaste's Mobile location.

"I asked him one question," Nelson said. "I said, 'Do you know how to transfer material from one vessel to another vessel without the material hitting the truck?' He told me that it couldn't be done."

The next day, Nelson proved the young man wrong. He put a hose into an empty vessel, ran the hose from the truck to a vessel filled with waste material, and vacuumed the material into the empty vessel. The truck was clean. Nelson's young protégé had learned a simple lesson about ingenuity that allowed him to grow and become a successful operations manager.

"I like to see challenges as opportunities. At Allwaste, I had more fun solving problems than I did getting good news. I'd always ask my people to tell me the bad news before the good so that we could help our customers solve their problems."

"At my retirement party in 1997, that kid cried like a baby," Nelson said. "That was a touching moment."

Not long ago, Nelson delivered a speech to Lake Charles, La., area high school seniors at McNeese State, which had recently recognized him as a distinguished alumnus. One of his talking points concerned proper conduct in business.

"I told them whatever you do, do it in an ethical manner," Nelson said. "That way when you go to sleep at night, you can put your head on the pillow without worrying about having taken advantage of anyone."

This attitude was instrumental to Allwaste's long-term success. Nelson tells the story of a job he and eight other Allwaste workers did in 1979 for Shell Oil. A ship had blown up at Shell's dock on the Houston Ship Channel, spilling oil into waters flowing toward the Gulf of Mexico. Nelson was one of 28 contractors working at the site to clean up the hideous mess. With so many different companies working frantically on that one job, organization was nonexistent. The brass at Shell, however, attempted to make the job as efficient as possible for the contractors.

"It was pandemonium," Nelson said. "Rather than having all the contractors' trucks leave the site every time they needed to fill up with gas or diesel, Shell supplied it to us."

The contractors could have easily left the site upon finishing the job without crediting Shell for its generosity on their invoices. Nelson, however, didn't believe it was the right thing to do.

"The purchasing agent who was in charge of the oilfield didn't know Shell was providing the gas and diesel," Nelson said. "When I brought my invoices in, I gave them credit for all the gas and diesel we used."

The credit amounted to $15,000. The purchasing agent was astonished at Nelson's honesty.

"Every contractor therein was asked how much gas and diesel they used," Nelson said. "They got so mad at me they couldn't see straight. But Shell ended up saving $250,000 that day."

While the good deed may have ruffled the feathers of his cohorts, it opened the door for repeat business from Shell that lasted through the end of Nelson's career.

* * *

Nelson now resides in Incline Village, Nev., with his wife Joan. The Nelsons are shown here with Joan's daughters Melissa Smith, left, and Heather Smith, right, and Bubba's daughter Mia Nelson.

Nelson now resides in Incline Village, Nev., (near Lake Tahoe) with his wife Joan. Although it's been a decade since he sold his beloved Allwaste, the entrepreneurial spirit is still alive within him. He recently invested in a seafood processing company in Texas called Hillman Shrimp and Oyster.

Just before the founding of Allwaste, Nelson, an avid golfer, set his clubs aside and didn't touch them for the next 20 years. His retirement in 1997 afforded him plenty of time to spend on the links, and he began competing in tournaments, including a national senior match play event that he won. In 2004, however, he suffered a stroke while vacationing in Turnberry, Scotland, and has not played since.

"It was a rude awakening for me because I attack golf like I attacked my business — all or nothing," Nelson said. "The bad thing about it is that I was a two handicap. If I had been an 18 handicap, it wouldn't have affected me as much."

Two years of extensive exercise and rehabilitation, however, have left Nelson in good health and spirits, and he looks forward to playing again very soon. His demeanor suggests that this latest challenge is viewed like any other he faced over the course of his career — as an opportunity rather than a setback.

"If I never play golf again, it won't be because I didn't put forth the effort!"

Whether it was a filthy incinerator or a creeping black ooze, Nelson never met a challenge he didn't like. As a matter of fact, he doesn't like the word "challenge" at all.

"It can have a negative connotation," Nelson said. "I like to see challenges as opportunities. At Allwaste, I had more fun solving problems than I did getting good news. I'd always ask my people to tell me the bad news before the good so that we could help our customers solve their problems."

A passion for helping people and a knack for solving problems are necessary traits for any entrepreneur, as Nelson's story shows. Combine those traits with vision, energy, professionalism and the support of well-rounded people, and you've got a formula for success.

R.E. "BOB"
PARKER
President
Repcon Inc.

There are several ways to get ahead in life. Some excel in their careers and personal lives through hard work, honesty, dedication and humility. Others strive for personal gain at any cost, whether that is respect, loyalty or even common decency.

Industrial construction entrepreneur R.E. "Bob" Parker sincerely hopes that future generations will follow the noble path more often than not — so much that he often speaks to high school and college students in the Corpus Christi, Texas, area about a proven recipe for success.

"I call it 'Uncle Bob's Dutch Uncle Talk,'" Parker said. "I don't talk to them about what supposedly makes a successful entrepreneur — I try to talk to them about life skills, dependability and doing what's right even if it's not popular."

That last talking point is a mantra for Parker, who founded Repcon Inc. — a maintenance and construction company that specializes in turnarounds, shutdowns and revamps for the chemical, refining and petrochemical industries — in 1983. The company's logo is always underlined by the phrase "We do things right!," whether it's written on stationery, business cards or coveralls. The words ring true, making up the core of a set of values that has enabled Repcon to turn a profit in every year of its existence while maintaining zero debt and achieving a safety record that has consistently been recognized by its peers in industry.

With a reputation like that, it would be easy for Parker to get up in front of those youngsters and say, "Try as hard as you can to be Bob Parker, and you will hit pay dirt." He believes, however, that anyone, regardless of intelligence, ability, age or heredity, can get as much as he wants out of life as long as he's willing to give it all he's got.

"I don't tell them what made me a successful businessman because I don't think I did anything special other than working hard and doing the right thing most of the time," Parker said. "When that happens, I believe you eventually succeed."

Having earned a degree in engineering from Texas A&I University (now Texas A&M University-Kingsville), Parker has special training in the art of decision making.

"The problem solving skills you learn in engineering are invaluable," Parker said. "I think that's the reason engineers make good managers. It's basic problem solving, and I don't mean two plus two equals four. You learn to rationally analyze and solve problems based on the resources you have available. Of course, there are lots of successful people who have no concept of engineering, but usually are still able to look at specific situations and make reasonably good judgments on what course should be taken."

Parker doesn't expect that most young people will become engineers just to learn how to distinguish a positive course of action from one that will result in failure. He does, however, encourage them to see how using good judgment in their formative years can alter the courses of their lives.

"One of the things plaguing society today is that most troubled people, whether they're alcoholics, drug addicts or car thieves, became that way because of bad decisions they made when they were younger," Parker said.

His assertion is not intended to be a condemnation of those who have made costly mistakes.

"A solid work ethic will overcome a lot of deficiencies, whether in brains or talent, or in terms of bad decisions you've made," Parker said. "If you work hard, you'll overcome that stuff."

* * *

Parker is well qualified to speak to others about such virtues. He's done the hard work and made the decisions necessary to achieve success at every stage of his career.

As a youth in Odem, Texas, Bob Parker spent lots of time working on farms.

As a youth growing up in Odem, Texas — a small town located north of Corpus Christi — Parker was never without responsibility. His father was the owner of a radio and television repair shop and a heating and air conditioning service center, and a farmer. Parker's parents expected their three boys to do chores around the house before and after school and wake up bright and early on Saturday mornings to work on the family farm.

"I grew up working around farm equipment and machinery," Parker said. "Beginning when I was 14 years old, I worked each summer for other farmers and for the local cotton gins and grain elevators. I liked machinery, and I made good grades in math and science, so my teachers and guidance counselors encouraged me to go into engineering."

Parker also began a relationship with a bank during his high school years that provided him with experience in borrowing and paying back loans.

"I raised pigs as a member of the Future Farmers of America," Parker said. "I would go down to the bank, borrow the money needed to run those projects and show the pigs, then sell them and pay off the loan. After that, I'd borrow money for the next year's project and do it over again."

His real-world education in finance would prove vital to pursuing a college degree.

"My parents told my brothers and I point blank that they could not pay for us to go to college," Parker said. "But they showed us things that we could do to make it happen."

According to Parker, engineering was not his first career choice.

"Originally I wanted to farm," Parker said. "But when I got out of high school, I realized my parents were not in a position to set me up in a farming operation. Farming requires a fairly large investment in land and equipment and most successful farmers got help from their families in getting started."

Parker took the advice of his teachers and counselors and enrolled in the general engineering program at Texas A&I, where he came under the tutelage of Dr. Marcus Truitt, a professor who also owned a surveying company. His relationship with Dr. Truitt led to a part-time job as a surveyor for the company that greatly enhanced Parker's education and work ethic.

"Dr. Truitt was probably the one who made me as anal as I am," Parker said. "He was very detail-oriented and expected absolute perfection from everyone who worked for him."

His job at Dr. Truitt's surveying company was just one of many Parker held during his college years. He worked weekends at a filling station owned by his uncle and at Texas A&I's campus bookstore. During the summers, Parker worked as a track man for Missouri Pacific Railroad, a rake man on an asphalt crew for B&E Construction and a project engineer for Blue Water Industries, and ran harvesting crews for various farmers in and around Odem. The money he earned was used to pay off loans he borrowed at the beginning of each school year for tuition and books.

Parker had established himself as a quick learner and a hard worker well before his college years. What began to emerge during his time working for Dr. Truitt, Missouri Pacific and B&E Construction, however, was his leadership ability.

"I was lucky to get a lot of varied experience working in different jobs for different employers," Parker said. "In almost every case, I ended up being promoted to supervisor or crew foreman. During the second summer that I worked for Missouri Pacific, they made me the foreman of an 'extra gang,' so I was in charge of my own 12-man crew. Dr. Truitt also put me in charge of all his surveying crews."

Parker attributes his tendency toward leadership not only to his headstrong nature but also his ability to engage and motivate people and his willingness to treat them with respect.

"When I've seen vacuums in positions ahead of me or to the side of me, I've always tended to move into them," Parker said. "I've never believed in getting ahead by trying to climb over the backs of other people. I try to practice one simple rule — treat other people the way you want to be treated. A manager should treat his employees the way he would want to be treated if he was in their shoes. If you do that consistently, you'll get results and you'll get respect. Do I slip up sometimes? Probably. But I truly believe the Golden Rule is the standard for leadership."

Of course, no leader can command respect without setting an example on the job.

"I think too many times people like to blow their own horns to get noticed by their bosses," Parker said. "It's much better just to quietly do

> *"I try to practice one simple rule — treat other people the way you want to be treated. If you do that consistently, you'll get results and respect."*

the job and let your work speak for itself. People are willing to follow good leaders that work as hard as their subordinates, so I always tried to set a good example by doing more than my share."

During his last year of college, Parker worked part-time for an engineering firm owned by Jimmy Goldston, who had previously managed Blue Water Industries. Parker went to work full-time for Goldston Corp. upon receiving his degree from Texas A&I.

"I started out in the Goldston engineering department, but later moved over to the construction side," Parker said. "At that time, all the company did was marine construction. We had tugboats and barges, and we did dock work and piledriving."

Parker was running a pile driving job for Goldston at a local refinery when an opportunity arose to expand the company's operations into industrial work. The result would prove to have a profound effect on Parker's career.

"The project manager who was running the project for the client asked if we could do some other things, such as structural steel and area paving," Parker said. "I didn't know that we couldn't, so I said, 'Sure.'"

Not long after the project was completed, Goldston purchased a small company called Refinery Maintenance Co. Parker, who had been with Goldston for less than three years, was named vice president and general manager of the new operating division and was given the opportunity to purchase the stock of Col. William Goldston — the original founder of the company — and become the second largest stockholder. He ran Refinery Maintenance Co. from 1974 until 1982, when economic conditions led to management changes at Goldston.

"Basically, the bottom had fallen out of the energy business," Parker said. "Our division was still generating consistent profits, but there were major differences of opinion on which way the company should go, primarily with the other operating divisions."

By mutual agreement, Parker sold the stock he owned in the company. Armed with a strong base of contacts and a decade of knowledge and training in the industry, Parker founded Repcon. For the first few months, the company consisted of Parker, his brother Sam and his long-time secretary Genie Lynn. The team was able to bring in more clients and began hiring additional employees. Repcon turned a small profit in its first full year of operation and has grown consistently ever since, maintaining strong relationships with plants all over North America and a sterling safety record.

* * *

In discussing the success of Repcon, Parker again alludes to his "Dutch Uncle" speech, the most avuncular element of which is probably the lesson about money management.

"I have always believed that you must live within your means," Parker said. "That's one of the key things I talk to the high school students about. I tell them that when you graduate, you shouldn't go out and buy a brand new car, rent a $1,500-per-month apartment and run up $5,000 in credit card debt when you're starting out with a $22,000-per-year salary. You may be able to handle it at first, but if you get sick and miss time at work, or if anything else goes wrong, you'll find yourself

106

digging out of a hole."

Parker has stood firm in his commitment to covering the basic needs of a functioning business and reinvesting profits.

"You have to figure out the absolute minimum you can survive on and make sure you've got that covered," Parker said. "I didn't have a lot of money when we started Repcon, but I had enough to where we could lease a facility and create new business. I'm not saying we have never had any bumps in the road, but we've never been in a situation where we've had to wonder if we're going to make the next payroll. Knowing the basic needs are covered makes you sleep better. And when there is a hiccup, it doesn't turn into a train wreck."

Parker founded Repcon Inc. in 1983. The company turned a small profit in its first full year of operation and has grown consistently ever since.

It's hard to imagine anything run by Parker turning into a catastrophe. Throughout his career, he has excelled by being dependable and working extra time to ensure that work gets done in the best way.

"You've got to be the guy whom the boss knows will be there every morning to do the job," Parker said. "Col. Goldston once said to me, 'I'm going to give you a piece of advice — you earn your salary in your first 40 hours, but you earn your promotions in your second 40 hours.' I sincerely believe that's true. Whether or not you have to work an entire 40 hours of overtime, the concept is the same."

During his talks, Parker asks the students who is the luckiest, the smartest and the biggest brown-noser of the group. Very few of the students ever admit to any of those distinctions.

"I ask them what would set any one of them apart if they all went to work for the same company, in the same department, doing the same job," Parker said. "Then I tell them the only thing that will get them recognized is to be the one who works hard, is dependable, and stands out for what he does, not for what he says about himself or what faults he points out in others."

To Parker, success comes in the moments when a person rises above normal expectations without fretting, complaining or making excuses.

"If you do that, you're going to be recognized for it, move up and eventually be the manager of your department," Parker said. "If you don't, you're going to be one of the multitude of people in the department 20 years down the road, wondering why everyone else got promoted over you. The kids relate to that."

Parker considers himself fortunate to make a living doing what he truly enjoys.

Parker's favorite anecdote is one that illustrates the competitiveness of the business world, in which survival is every bit as important a pursuit as it is in the wilderness.

"There are two guys walking in the woods, and they come across a bear," Parker says. "One of the guys sits down and starts taking off his shoes. The other guy says, 'What are you doing? You can't outrun that bear!' The first guy says, 'I don't need to outrun the bear. I just need to outrun you.'"

Each time he relates that story to an audience, Parker sees light bulbs flashing above the heads of the listeners. Parker no doubt learned a similar lesson during his days as a young laborer, and he still preaches it to his team members to this day.

"When we're on a project, other contractors are there also," Parker said. "You always have some things that don't go perfectly on a project, but if everybody else has worse things going on or is farther behind schedule, that's where the heat is. So that's the concept we use. You do the absolute best you can, but you don't have to outrun the bear."

Staying ahead of the competition has served Repcon well. Encountering problems is an unavoidable part of business. How those issues are addressed and dealt with often means the difference between success and failure.

Although Parker didn't get the chance to pursue his original objective of becoming a career farmer, he is quite happy with the course he's taken in life. When asked about his hobbies, Parker said that while he enjoys golf and bird hunting, there are few things he'd rather do than grow and maintain the success of Repcon and its people.

"I'm extremely fortunate to make a living doing something I truly enjoy," Parker said. "I could be doing something totally different, but I believe that no matter what that was, I would have worked hard and tried to be successful at it."

In other words, regardless of the path he chose, Parker would most likely have ended up with a great lesson to impart to America's future leaders about fulfilling their dreams. The winning formula is clear, and it doesn't take the education of an engineer or the business acumen of a wealthy entrepreneur to see what actions and attitudes will yield success.

JOHN MICHAEL
PAZ
President & CEO
Godwin Pumps

In the late '50s, future Paz Brothers Construction co-founder John Paz witnessed an event that changed his perspective on his career. Back then, he was an ironworker, doing jobs at industrial plants in an era when there was less emphasis on workplace safety.

One day, he witnessed a co-worker suffering from a shaking fit while standing on a scaffold that had been erected near a very high chimney stack. As Paz watched the man teeter at the top of the scaffold, he had a choice to make — either wait for someone else to rescue him or do it himself. He was forced to choose the latter option when he discovered that the only other ironworker on the job had been drinking alcohol and was not in a position to be a hero. Paz sprung into action, scaling the scaffold and bringing his co-worker to safety.

Paz's boss vowed to reward him with a raise and a promotion. For the young laborer, however, no reward — financial or otherwise — or personal acclaim could convince him to remain in a situation where responsible leadership was lacking.

Fifty years later, Paz's son John Michael, president & CEO of Godwin Pumps, likes to tell this anecdote to illustrate the high expectations his father held not only for the attitudes and behaviors of others but also for his own life.

"My father realized he needed to work for himself because his principles and his work ethic were higher than what he was able to find in others," John Michael said. "He was a natural entrepreneur, the kind of person who was always looking to see how he could create his own success."

Just 26 years of age, Paz quit his job and founded a heavy construction company with his brothers Ted, 28, and Bob, 19. The three young entrepreneurs started their business with nothing but a bulldozer purchased from money borrowed from their father and from a bank, and began to bid jobs. The trio possessed a strong aptitude for business and an extraordinary work ethic, and over the next five decades, Paz Brothers Construction enjoyed consistent success.

Paz passed away Aug. 12, 2006, at his home in Mickleton, N.J., after a bout with cancer. Described by his son as a charismatic man who enjoyed countless friendships and fruitful business partnerships, Paz's legacy will endure through the memories of the many people on which he made an impact. He bequeathed an intangible inheritance to his son as he left this world — the spirit of entrepreneurship. (In addition to Paz Brothers, Paz founded a construction equipment leasing company, co-founded a carbon water filtration venture and operated a restaurant in Atlantic City, N.J., among other businesses.)

Whether that spirit was handed down through DNA or learned through observation, it is strong within John Michael, who has grown Godwin Pumps to a $200-million-plus-per-year, worldwide operation since he took it over nearly three decades ago.

* * *

The story of Godwin Pumps begins in the mid-'70s, when John Michael was a junior studying business at Dickinson College in Carlisle, Penn. Ironically, it was a Paz family vacation that led to the company's founding.

"My dad called me one day and told me he was planning a trip to England for himself and my mother," John Michael said. "He asked me to go because he was looking at the viability of bringing pumps manufactured by a small British company to the United States."

The idea of traveling abroad excited John Michael. Though he'd had opportunities to do so as part of his college curriculum, he passed on them in order to fulfill his responsibilities as a leader in his fraternity. He accepted his father's invitation, however, and the family spent an entire week in the month of November both vacationing and researching diesel-driven pumps. During their time in England, they visited a pump factory operated by a small company by the name of H.J. Godwin.

"We met with the managing director and had a wonderful visit," John Michael said. "We went to some banks to set up credit, and within a couple of weeks of returning home, we had made a deal with Godwin to import complete

John Paz, right, formed Godwin Pumps of America after visiting the H.J. Godwin pump factory during a family vacation in England. Also pictured are his son John Michael, left, and his wife Barbara.

diesel-driven pumps on a 40-foot container into the port of Philadelphia."

Paz formed a new company known as Godwin Pumps of America in 1976 as a result of the partnership. He found a partner and enlisted the help of his son, who had yet to complete his education. John Michael worked for Godwin during the summer between his junior and senior years. Before he could earn his degree, however, his future would begin to take shape.

"My dad expressed to me his belief in Godwin's potential, but he also told me things weren't working out with his partner," John Michael said. "He needed someone to grab it and run with it, and he wanted me to consider that."

John Michael had planned to pursue a law degree after receiving his bachelor's degree. His father had always been very emphatic about the importance of getting a good education, and it surprised him to hear Paz encourage him to forego law school in order to help run Godwin. John Michael visited the professors he respected the most to gauge their opinions on his options.

"They agreed unanimously that I should take the opportunity to go into business for myself," John Michael said. "They reasoned that I could go back to school later on if I wanted to."

John Michael joined Godwin in 1978 and Paz appointed him as its president in 1985. From the beginning, the task of running what was essentially a side business of his father's was a challenge.

"When I took over the company, I was working out of my father's office at Paz Brothers," John Michael said. "To this day, they were some of the most trying times of my career. It never seemed like it was going to be what I envisioned."

John Michael had great expectations for Godwin. He saw a future in which the company would expand beyond its territory along the Eastern seaboard and sell pumps all over the United States. He knew, however, that he would have to earn it.

"I realized early on that it wasn't going to be easy," John Michael said. "Also, all of my friends and classmates from Dickinson College were graduating from law school, getting MBAs and becoming doctors. My roommate got a job working for Georgia-Pacific as a vice president."

Feeling bound to what he calls a "quasi-family business" in his hometown while his best friends flourished in big cities all over the Northeast, John Michael began to question his decision. Never one to back away from a challenge, however, he put his reservations aside and worked as hard as he could to build Godwin into a success he could call his own.

Eight years later, that dream was realized. John Michael built a brand new facility for himself and his team of seven staff members four miles down the road from the Paz Brothers office. Sales had increased fivefold since he became president, but the feeling of independence was more gratifying.

"I can't say that I wasn't driven by money," John Michael said. "But I loved what I did, and my goal was to sell Godwin pumps — it wasn't just to get rich. I was more concerned with being successful at what I did, and I knew if I did that, the rest would take care of itself."

John Michael Paz had great expectations for Godwin Pumps when he joined the company in 1978. He saw a future in which it would expand beyond its territory along the Eastern seaboard and sell pumps all over the United States.

Once Godwin Pumps of America had physically established itself as an independent entity, profits began to grow exponentially. John

Michael began to hire more people with diverse and complementary skills and found new ways to expand the business. By 1989, he had found a way for Godwin to begin importing parts from England and assembling pumps at the company's factory rather than importing complete pumps. As the success of Godwin ballooned, John Michael ramped up his efforts to sell in new territories, relying on his team to maintain the company's momentum on a day-to-day basis.

"I had them all over for dinner one night and said, 'Gang, we're doing great, but I want to make this a nationwide operation,'" John Michael said. "I told them that in order for us to do that, I would have to

> *"When you're an entrepreneur, and you have an idea, pick a course of action and go with it. Do the best you can and make it what you want it to be. You're not going to find the perfect scenario. You find something you love and work at it to make it the best it can be."*

be away more often figuring out how to make it happen, and that they'd have to pick up some of my work."

The group responded with a resounding vote of confidence. John Michael hit the road, working trade shows and building relationships with distributors. The first Godwin Pumps branch office was opened in Maryland in 1989, kicking off a decade of expansion that would culminate in the fulfillment of John Michael's ultimate goal of becoming the sole distributor of Godwin Pumps in the United States. In 2001, John Michael acquired the H.J. Godwin factory in England, which had been sold to a venture capitalist, and Godwin has expanded to nearly every continent in the world since then. It now employs more than 750 people around the world.

In 2005, John Michael was named Entrepreneur of the Year for the Philadelphia and Eastern Pennsylvania region by Ernst & Young. During his acceptance speech, he gave considerable credit for his success to a true mentor — his mother Barbara, who was a homemaker until her mid-40s, when she decided to pursue studies in education and child development.

"I learned a lot of things from her," John Michael said. "She used to say to me, 'Where there's a will, there's a way.' She also taught me that we should always make decisions rather than hesitating or not deciding at all. Move forward — if it's the wrong decision, you can always fix it later."

According to John Michael, following his mother's sage advice has led to success in his professional life and inspiration beyond.

"When you're an entrepreneur, and you have an idea, pick a course of action and go with it," John Michael said. "Do the best you can and make it what you want it to be. You're not going to find the perfect scenario. You find something you love and work at it to make it the best it can be."

John Michael feels as though he's there. He employs a staff of hardworking, compassionate individuals, many of whom have been at his side for more than 20 years. His boundless energy and enthusiasm have no doubt left an impression on his team members, just as his father's visions of success permeated his consciousness when he was a boy. He confesses to having a special place in his heart for people who started their careers under the tutelage of their fathers.

"I like finding people who tell me that they worked on their fathers' farms or in their fathers' small businesses," John Michael said. "They tend to take a lot of pride in their work because they've been driven by the desire to make their fathers proud and to help them be successful."

Surely John Paz took pride in the fact that his son rose to the challenge of jumping into a new business immediately after graduating from college. Having been raised in the countryside of southern New Jersey by Polish immigrants, nothing ever came easy for the elder Paz. As a young teenager, Paz drew inspiration from his older brother

116

Michael, who joined the military at the age of 17 and served in World War II as a flight engineer.

"He always coveted his brother's love and affection," John Michael said. "My uncle would always fight his battles for him and things like that."

Michael flew alongside a famous B-17 captain by the name of McCullough in the Pacific theatre. He earned nine medals, including the Distinguished Flying Cross. On his very last mission, however, he was killed in an accident. It affected Paz immensely, perhaps motivating him to be a hero in the business world, whether it was through saving the life of a co-worker, leading Paz Brothers Construction when his older brother and best friend Ted died at age 42, or setting the stage for his son's success as an entrepreneur.

Just before he passed, Paz was taken on a final trip to England by his son aboard a Falcon 50 jet owned by Godwin. (Aviation has always been a hobby for John Michael, who owns and manages his own airplanes.) As the two men had coffee together during the flight, Paz took a moment to reflect on everything he and his son had achieved — two very successful enterprises, a bevy of awards, material wealth, an enduring family legacy — and put it all into perspective with a few simple words.

"He looked at me and he said, 'Can you believe this? Not bad for a couple of farm boys from New Jersey,'" John Michael said.

NICKY
PREJEAN
President & CEO
Southland Fire & Safety Equipment

"When you hear the music, don't just stand there. Get up and dance or go home."

Nicky Prejean is a 30-plus-year veteran of the industrial fire safety and equipment industry — hardly the résumé of anyone who knows anything about dancing. The founder, president and CEO of Southland Fire & Safety Equipment in Gonzales, La., can't teach you to two-step. He won't lead you in a waltz or swing you 'round and 'round. As a matter of fact, the last thing you'll get when you deal with the straight-shooting Prejean is a song-and-dance routine.

His analogy is meant to illustrate his approach to business. Acting and reacting in times of opportunity and challenge are vital to the success of an entrepreneur. If there's any situation that can make a human being so mentally, emotionally and physically nimble, it's a fire.

Experiences with fire in the late '60s and early '70s proved inspirational to the young and hard-working Prejean. An old Borg-Warner Chemicals newsletter from 1976 tells the story of how he reacted to an industrial fire while working as a maintenance employee for Cos-Mar in Geismar, La.

"A story continues to prevail that on one occasion, when an emergency alarm was sounded at Cos-Mar, Nicky was the first person over the Mississippi River levee located about a quarter of a mile south of the plant," reads the article, titled "How to Make a Million $ or Race You to the Levee."

The image of Prejean running for dear life at the sound of a fire alarm is both funny and ironic considering his current status as a legend in his industry. But instead of branding young Nicky a coward, we should commend him for using the experience as motivation to enter a new and rewarding phase in his career.

"As a result of the fire, the plant decided to train us to overcome the fear and build our confidence," Prejean said. "It got me very familiar with the equipment and made me appreciate the need for training in the petrochemical industry."

Prejean became so interested in industrial fire training that he became an instructor, teaching personnel at Texas A&M University, the LSU Fire & Emergency Training Institute (FETI) and at industrial sites across the Gulf Coast. During that time, he was able to learn at the feet of LSU FETI instructors Bill Cromwell and Marvin Crowe, both of whom Prejean names as mentors. They instilled in him everything from expertise in training personnel and maintaining fire safety equipment to work ethics.

Prejean already knew a bit about business management. He had for a few years sold and repaired lawnmowers and go-carts, in addition to owning a beauty salon operated by his wife Muriel. Although his experiences in training no doubt planted the seeds for his entry into the fire and safety equipment business, a small blaze at his lawnmower repair and go-cart shop set the wheels in motion. In a world without home maintenance megastores, fire extinguishers were hard to come by, especially in 1970 Gonzales. Forced to order an extinguisher through Cos-Mar's safety director, Prejean saw an opportunity to provide a service to his community and make money at the same time. He and a friend by the name of Steve Robert opened their own fire extinguisher shop in a barn, investing only $100.

Fire extinguisher sales took off, but the success story truly began when customers started to request service on their equipment. Three years later, the 27-year-old Prejean made another dash from the plant, this time toward the fulfillment of the great American dream — he quit his job at Cos-Mar and officially went into business for himself.

120

* * *

It's been said that consistently successful individuals and groups remain so because they are able to put their greatest achievements behind them, thereby eluding complacency.

Southland Fire & Safety Equipment experienced a tenfold increase in profits in just three years, and has enjoyed consistent business from industry in the Gulf South ever since. (The company now operates out of three locations — Gonzales, Port Allen and Norco, La.) In the early days, Prejean worked alongside industry legends such as Red Adair and Boots and Coots — quite a privilege for an up-and-coming fire safety professional at that time.

Thirty-four years later, Prejean still runs Southland Fire & Safety Equipment as though it's Year Zero. In an organization of about 50 people, he's the only person who's always on call. Over the years, he has earned a reputation among his peers and colleagues in Ascension Parish for dependability.

If a conflagration breaks out at a plant on Christmas Eve, Prejean will rush to the scene on request. Surely his family understands and appreciates his dedication — his sons Bert, Brett and Bart and daughter Tonia Sheets all hold positions within the company. (Bert manages fire truck maintenance, repair and fabrication, works in industrial and petrochemical sales, and is a first responder; Bart manages the company's Port Allen location; Brett is the company's Gonzales business manager; and Tonia is an industrial sales representative.)

Nicky Prejean, right, learned at the feet of Louisiana State University Fire & Emergency Training Institute instructor Marvin Crowe and others whom he considers to be his mentors.

Although the future of the company seems set with so many

Prejeans holding important posts, it is apparent to any observer that the father of the clan is and has always been the driving force.

According to his children, life wasn't easy during the early days of Southland Fire & Safety Equipment.

"Dad was always gone during our childhood, which made it seem as though he was neglecting his children," Bert Prejean said. "But he worked very hard throughout his life to see to it that we would have something when we were older. Now that his children have children of their own, he gives the grandkids every moment he can. He has a lot more free time than he did when we were growing up."

"One thing that I have always admired about him is the way he turned the family around from utter poverty and hard times," Brett Prejean said. "On some days, it feels like he runs our family with an iron fist. I think that's a direct response to being raised differently himself. I often joke to my friends that we live in a communist system, and King Nicky is our leader."

Brett claims that his father has become more gentle with age. Employees describe him as being kind, personable, quick-witted, eager to help and always concerned with the safety and security of those who help maintain his company's success. He's less dictatorial these days, but Prejean has remained omniscient in all things related to the business.

"I always tell people that my dad is the smartest man I know," Brett said. "He doesn't come across as an intellectual, but seems to know a lot about many things. He always knows everything that's going on in the company, even when he is not here."

His leadership has been particularly vital in recent years, as large companies have put extra pressure on family-owned businesses like Southland Fire & Safety Equipment to compete. According to friends, employees and colleagues, Prejean is the type of man who succeeds even under the most adverse circumstances. He has proved this time and again over the course of his career.

"The idea that a small mom and pop organization can't do well is a myth," Prejean said. "When the owners get old and give up, those organizations tend to go away. I hope it doesn't happen here, but there's no guarantee. I think where there's a will, there's a way."

"You've got to provide a service that's needed and you've got to do it well."

It goes without saying that fire protection is needed in industry. Doing it well is almost certainly more complicated than most people think, but Prejean believes the only other option is failure, and thus destruction, injury and death.

Expertise and personalized service have been among the keys to quality work since Southland's inception. Prejean prides himself on working without supply contracts and by offering a wide inventory of equipment, which eliminates the need for catalog sales. When asked why com-

"Life is filled with peaks and valleys. Some days you can jump over a building, and other days you can stumble over flat ground. On the days that I feel like I can jump over a building, I try to do as much as I can."

petitors haven't caught on to that formula, the modest Prejean attributes it to good luck.

"It's difficult for them to copy the motion of this company because they can't copy me," Prejean said. "We started it on a grassroots level and it built up with significant overhead. Most of our sales are for specialty items. Having worked mechanical in a plant, I feel like I recognize the need for those types of things. Historically the fire and safety equipment industry has been kind of a mail-order business. But the companies that have supply contracts often can't get the equipment to their customers quickly enough.

"I don't know how long that will last," Prejean added. "It's lasted 10 years longer than I thought it would!"

Over the years, Southland has had a number of opportunities to buy competing businesses. In 1985, Prejean purchased Fire Equipment and Maintenance in Port Allen — which to this day is the company's outpost in that area — for what he describes as "peanuts." Otherwise, he has been wary of taking on projects that require more time and ability than he and his gifted, hardworking team possess.

"If the previous owners tried it and it wasn't working, I figured I couldn't do it either," Prejean said. "I'd rather do what I do and get better at it."

* * *

Casual observers may view Prejean as a living example of how keeping a singular focus can lead to success. That's true to an extent, but it may surprise some to learn that he has diverse interests outside Southland Fire & Safety Equipment, though work is never sacrificed for play.

In the early '60s, when Bert Prejean was just four years old, Nicky and a neighbor who also had a young son decided to build a go-cart for their boys. Somewhere along the assembly line, however, the objective changed.

"By the time the go-cart got built, I enjoyed riding it more than anyone else," Nicky said. "From that first stage, we forgot about the kids, and the daddies started to ride."

Prejean developed what would turn out to be a lifelong interest in stock car racing. It wasn't long before he was attending NASCAR events. His interest in professional racing culminated in an unexpected job offer — while attending a race in Prairieville, La., he was approached by a NASCAR official and asked to be a flagman. For the next five years, Prejean traveled across the Gulf South flagging races for the nation's premier league, including the Daytona 500. When he grew weary of being on the road so often, he relinquished his duties as a flagman and purchased his own racing car.

"I didn't plan to race it — just to look at it," he joked.

That plan failed when Prejean received a call from local racer Freddie Fryer, whose own car was no longer serviceable after a crash. It was the beginning of his very own NASCAR team, which won 70 percent of the races in which it competed. Prejean is credited with helping to launch the career of NASCAR legend Rusty Wallace, who was a member and a partner in the team for several years.

Increased time demands forced Prejean to give up on NASCAR in 1987.

"I either had to get out of that or get out of my business," he said. "The business was more of a sure thing."

Not that Prejean has invested only in sure things. Two years after leaving NASCAR, he was persuaded by a friend to go in on the purchase of a local bank.

"I had no desire to do it because everyone I knew in that business was either broke or in jail," he said.

Prejean, his friend and another partner purchased the bank for $1 million. In 11 years, they grew its assets from $25 million to $100 million. Prejean reluctantly served as the chairman of the board for the bank before its ultimate sale. Even though he had no experience in the banking industry, he came out of the deal having made a considerable profit in a relatively short period of time.

"I don't like to fool with things that are so heavily scrutinized by the government," Prejean said. "I never did want to get caught up in scandals for which I had no personal responsibility. In the fire and safety equipment business, we have to adhere to many regulations, and I have to depend on about 20 of my people to make sure we do so. There's a lot of risk associated with that, but there's a reward for doing it and not experiencing any misfortunes."

While NASCAR and the banking industry may have taken Prejean out of his comfort zone to varying degrees, industry-oriented extracurricular activities have enhanced his career. He was instrumental to the formation of a local HazMat team that includes industrial workers and law enforcement officials. He is a member of many associations, including the Ascension Parish Chamber of Commerce, the Louisiana Emergency Preparedness Association, the Louisiana Chemical Alliance and others. He has also made generous donations to local schools and nonprofit organizations.

This isn't to say that his racing and banking ventures were detrimental to his success. If anything, Prejean's good track record both inside and outside his company proves that you can spread yourself just a little and not lose sight of what's important, no matter how demanding your livelihood may be.

A great example of this is his service on the Louisiana Regional Airport Authority. During the early '80s, a controversial plan to build an airport in Ascension Parish was conceived by local leaders. Joe Sevario, a state senator at the time, was charged with appointing a committee leader to spearhead the plan, which many residents didn't approve of due to safety concerns. Seeking a well-known business leader in the parish with a reputation for getting things done, Sevario turned to Prejean, whom he'd known since early childhood.

"He pursues things 100 percent," Sevario once said of Prejean. "He's a common guy who has accomplished a lot of uncommon goals."

After years of legal wranglings, bureaucratic hurdles and board meetings that took place in hotel restaurants, tin buildings and even poorly lit parking lots, the airport was built. Many people doubted that it could be done, but Prejean never gave up, perhaps motivated more by the collective opinion of the naysayers than anything else. He served on the board of directors for many years, then left before returning recently to assist with expansion projects. In the summer of 2006, he was appointed chairman of the Ascension/St. James Airport & Transportation Authority by Louisiana Gov. Kathleen Blanco.

* * *

"Once a man called me wanting to get a price on putting out a fire," Prejean said. "I thought that was kind of a silly question because there were too many unknowns. I just told him, 'If you need to ask that question, you probably can't afford our services.'"

There's nothing like good old honesty. Unwilling to put a price on the safety of a human life, Prejean has instilled the belief among his customers and team members that only the best possible service is sufficient. That's just one of many reasons why Southland has managed to remain successful without ever having to obtain a business loan or go public.

Prejean spends time with his grandsons Cole, Holden and Mason.

"The public companies we deal with are dependent on the Dow Jones, a board of directors and shareholders," Prejean said. "It can take a board of directors weeks to make a decision. I control all of it, so I can make a decision in a minute."

Prejean strongly encourages budding entrepreneurs to strive for financial independence if possible and avoid purchases that stretch their means.

"My advice is to not borrow money — you have to pay that back," he said. "And before I spend $20,000 on a vehicle, I like to put that money in a box and look at it for a day or two. Then I decide whether I want it or the vehicle."

It doesn't shock the listener to hear Prejean say that things have been remarkably stable at Southland Fire & Safety Equipment during its three decades of existence. What is surprising is his refusal to brand the company as a true success story. In his mind, the fortunes of today don't necessarily guarantee similar returns tomorrow.

"Life is filled with peaks and valleys," he said. "Some days you can jump over a building, and other days you can stumble over flat ground. On the days that I feel like I can jump over a building, I try to do as much as I can."

Prejean's bad days are probably more productive than the good days of many successful people. Still, he finds plenty of time to spend at home in Lake Martin, La., or at his river camp with his wife (a well-known painter in Ascension Parish), his four children and his five grandchildren. Although his NASCAR years are far behind him, he now owns a drag racing team managed by his son Bert. He also breeds horses, and occasionally finds the time to produce local musicians.

Maybe he does know something about dancing after all.

R. DEWON
RANKIN
Founder
HRI Inc.

As the old saying goes, if you can't stand the heat, stay out of the kitchen. No entrepreneur, however, can claim to have achieved success without ever breaking a sweat.

In the days before personal protective equipment (PPE) became a standard in industry, boilermakers simply held their breath while working in high-heat environments and cooled their feet off with water afterward.

Those days of daring came to an end during the early '90s when OSHA mandated the use of PPE in confined spaces.

R. Dewon Rankin, a longtime boilermaker from Missouri, spent most of his career doing things the old-fashioned way. But when the new OSHA regulations were enacted, he saw a clear opportunity to revolution-ize the way hot work was performed.

For many years, Dewon had been thinking of new ways to protect workers in high-temperature environments. Although he had no experi-ence in developing personal protective equipment, he decided to enlist the help of his sons Roger and Curt — a boilermaker and a crop consultant, respectively — to research materials that could be used to make heat-resistant clothing.

"I realized there was a need for this kind of service, and so we worked continuously to fulfill that need," Dewon said.

With the help of carpenter Jeff Enlund, the Rankins constructed a 500-degree test booth on their farm near Buffalo, Mo., and began experi-menting with a variety of materials.

"We made contacts within the clothing industry prior to getting started," Curt said. "We consulted with them on what types of materials and insulations could work, and would buy samples to do our own testing and evaluation."

The Rankins began their research in 1987 with proximity suits, which are commonly used by fire departments when fighting flash fires. They set criteria for the materials they tested, assessing their comfort and endurance and whether they allowed the worker to crawl through small entryways. Described by his brother as the team's "action" man, Roger accepted the challenge of putting his own personal safety on the line in order to see the project to its fruition.

"I was the test child," Roger said. "I didn't care — I was in my early 20s, and I thought I was bulletproof."

In order to ensure that the equipment met OSHA standards, the Rankins hired an agency representative to critique the work being done at the test site. After years of trial and error, they developed heat-, steam- and flame-resistant equipment consisting of an outer layer of aluminized carbon-Kevlar, a moisture barrier and fireproof coveralls. The equipment also included a respirator, a back-up air bottle, a personal air conditioner and a bone mike, which enabled communication between workers.

The Rankins started High-Temp Repair and Inspection (HRI) Inc. in 1993 with the goal of building a clientele of industrial plants seeking

safe, efficient maintenance and repair in hazardous conditions. As is the case with many startup businesses, success didn't come overnight.

"Anything worth doing takes a while," Curt said. "We didn't even start doing field work until 1996."

With Dewon providing vision and driving sales, and his sons managing the business and operations, HRI began to make inroads during the late '90s. One particular job at an oil refinery in Wood River, Ill., proved to be a major turning point for the fledgling company. The mission was to

From left (front row), Curt, Dewon and Roger Rankin founded High-Temp Repair and Inspection (HRI) Inc. in 1993. Also pictured is HRI partner Jeff Enlund, who has worked with the Rankins since before the company's inception.

130

repair a secondary external cyclone in a cat cracker that had been punctured.

"By the time we were called in, the hole was substantially large," Roger said. "If a catalyst line gets a hole in it, it erodes the material on the line by the hour. It's just like taking a water hose to a bank of sand."

In most cases, the cat cracker unit would have to be shut down. HRI's crew, however, repaired the stainless steel cyclone in 1,200-degree heat over a period of three weeks.

"We ended up building a box around two cyclones, and they never had to shut the unit down," Roger said. "It was very costly to us. The client's safety record was very good at that time, and it was a credit to us that we completed that project and kept the cat unit from shutting down."

HRI was founded with the goal of building a clientele of industrial plants seeking safe, efficient maintenance and repair in hazardous conditions.

Although the job put HRI on the map, the intense heat resulted in the destruction of nearly all the company's equipment. Since all the equipment is made in house, the Rankins and their team were able to recover in a relatively short period of time. Still, this "trial by fire" of sorts was a wake-up call.

"You never know what you're going to get in that type of environment," Curt said. "We were prepared to make repairs and replace parts, but it happened a little sooner than we expected. It was a challenging experience, but it really got us working."

* * *

Destructive heat wasn't the only obstacle faced by HRI in its early days. Potential customers were initially skeptical of the company's attempt to break new ground in industry.

"In the beginning we were viewed as radicals," Roger said. "People didn't understand the technology and the equipment and how it protected the individual."

Roger admits that even he questioned the viability of the operation at times.

"Anytime you create a market for new products, and you're not making any money, you have second thoughts," he said. "An entrepreneur has to be an optimist, but that's not to say that you don't have doubts every now and then."

Curt and Roger will always credit their father, whose boundless energy and never-say-die attitude pushed HRI toward success, as their mentor.

The Rankins and their crew members, however, banded together and worked hard to meet the high expectations of their customers. HRI success stories were being created with each new job, and by 2002, the company's method was well-established and widely recognized in the refining and power industries of North America.

"We got the buy-in of management at facilities when our crews performed work much more quickly than their own people did," Roger said. "Once people saw our work and how safe it was, they became more comfortable."

HRI complemented its technical skill with honesty and reliability, values instilled by Dewon in his sons and passed along to the company's crew members.

"That's how we approached our business," Curt said. "When you start something, you have to be upfront with people and tell them the truth. For instance, most of the time you can help a customer, but there are also times when you can't. If an HRI foreman tells a customer we can help, we're here to stand by him and do our best to make it happen that way."

The ability to make things happen was a product of Dewon's vast experience. Since he had spent most of his career working with companies like Johnson Controls, Riley Stoker and Foster Wheeler, Dewon learned firsthand the value of high-temperature work and the importance of safety and procedures. The dream of becoming an entrepreneur began on the family farm, but for Dewon and his sons, the research never really concluded.

"My advice to anyone would be to learn your job thoroughly and continue learning on a daily basis," Dewon said.

Dewon recently retired from HRI, leaving Roger to run the field operations as company president and Curt, who holds a minor in business, as its secretary-treasurer. (Enlund, who is now vice president, takes care of HRI's equipment and manages the shop.) The Rankin brothers learn new things about running a successful business with each passing day. Roger, for instance, has learned that it's better to trust people who can fill niches within a company than to assume tasks.

"You have to realize you're not a professional in every field,"

> *"My advice to anyone would be to learn your job thoroughly and continue learning on a daily basis."*

Roger said. "I think a lot of people try do things they should hire other people for due to a lack of capital or other reasons. That was a lesson we learned very early on."

Both men acknowledge that entrepreneurship isn't consistently gratifying. Nothing ever comes easy, and for this reason, the brothers approach every job like it's the most important HRI has ever done.

"I try to keep a positive attitude and make the right decisions," Roger said. "Entrepreneurship is a long row to hoe. It's not for everyone. A lot of people don't want to do anything beyond 8 to 5. There's no instant satisfaction for an entrepreneur — it's hard work all the way through."

"We all have our ups and downs," Curt added. "But the one thing that's remained consistent is our desire to grow HRI and keep it running."

Dewon now spends most of his time pursuing a lifelong passion — tending to his farm. He displays registered show cattle at events such as the Tulsa State Fair and the Houston Livestock Show & Rodeo. His sons, both of whom are married and have two children apiece, raise beef cattle in their down time.

"I love to see things growing," Dewon said. "Whether it's plants, vegetables or our company, I receive great pleasure from watching the growth process."

Curt and Roger will always credit their father, whose boundless energy and never-say-die attitude pushed HRI toward success, as their mentor.

"He's an old-school construction guy, always working nose-to-the-ground and tearing it up," Roger said. "His persistence and drive resulted in positive cash flow for our business. It just so happened that Curt and I were able to fill the other parts of it and help make it happen."

The Rankins' innovation in the field of high-temperature repair is symbolic of their road to success. Though the conditions haven't always been favorable to growth and progress, Dewon, Roger and Curt have worn their determination and commitment to quality like a suit of armor. No amount of heat — whether generated by a cat cracker or a naysayer — can destroy that.

FORREST
SHOOK
President & CEO
NLB Corp.

"I've always wanted to provide quality products, take risks and look for opportunities to make some money," said Forrest Shook, founder and CEO of NLB Corp., a leading manufacturer of high-pressure and ultrahigh-pressure waterjetting equipment. "I soon found that to do this you must have the passion and strength to follow through and keep fighting to build and create every day. When you stop doing this, it's the day the business is going to start dying."

The quote above doesn't read like the testimony of a man whose life as an entrepreneur began in an office located in the middle of a junkyard in Flint, Mich., with a single employee — a lanky wino who hailed from the roughest part of town — and no customers. But when you consider that only a fellow of such moxie could have risen from those humble beginnings to become a wealthy entrepreneur, it seems very appropriate.

According to Shook, his passion for entrepreneurship began at age 12, when he raised rabbits and chickens to sell to a local butcher shop and peddled sweet corn on the side of a highway. He first started to take interest in high-pressure equipment in his early 20s, when he assembled a pressure washer with a water tank, a hot water heater, a 600-psi pump driven by a Wisconsin engine and a portable generator purchased from the local Sears department store. Shook used the portable pressure washer, which was mounted in an 18-foot van truck, to clean trucks, buildings and construction machinery around Flint.

His first company, Flint Mobil Wash, began after he secured a

$5,000 loan from his wary parents.

"It took me about three or four months to convince them that I wasn't crazy," Shook said.

By the time Shook manufactured his original pressure washer, he had only $67 left to his name. Undaunted, he left home and moved into the junkyard office, which doubled as living quarters.

"It wasn't a pretty situation, but I was bound and determined to make it work," Shook said. "The pressure to make my monthly payments was intense. I don't remember how many hot dogs I ate during that time, but it was a lot. It was about all I could afford."

The steady diet of dogs and determination was just enough for Shook to get by for a couple of years. Things began to pick up when Shook took advantage of opportunities to clean gas stations, houses and other various types of buildings. He moved into a mobile home (his idea of a palace at that time) and began to seek out pumps with higher pressure, which would allow him to complete the jobs at a faster pace.

"At about that time I received a call from a man by the name of Gil Mains, who was a former Detroit Lions football player," Shook said. "He was building a truck stop in Dearborn, Mich., and wanted to install a drive-through truck wash. I helped him do that while I was operating my company."

During the course of his work with car washes, Shook got the idea to manufacture a urethane-style roller that could be used to push a car through a wash on a double-chain conveyor. This eliminated the need for a person to hook the car up to a chain in order to pull it through. Shook began to manufacture that product, which he called Lube Roller, and later started a car wash soap manufacturing business called Mainline Chemical. On top of all that, he started another pressure washer manufacturing company called S&T Equipment Co.

Forrest Shook founded his first company, Flint Mobil Wash, in his early 20s after securing a loan from his parents.

"By the time I was 25 years old, I owned or was a partner in five individual companies," Shook said. "It was a struggle to try to make all these companies profitable. After a few years of trying to juggle all those balls in the air, I came to realize that it wasn't working."

Shook decided to sell Flint Mobil Wash, for which he only got a few thousand dollars, and shut down Lube Roller, Mainline Chemical and S&T Equipment Co. He vowed to focus all his time and effort on his next venture, whatever that might be.

* * *

Shortly after marrying his wife Delores and moving into a house, Shook began to envision a company that would manufacture and sell 10,000-psi pumps. This new venture — which he started after refinancing his house and receiving $2,000 from an accountant named John Stimson, who was a minority stock holder for several years — was originally called

"I found out a long time ago that if you can't build quality products and fulfill the needs of your customers, you will not be successful."

National Liquid Blasting. In the first year, National Liquid Blasting netted sales of $87,000, yielding a profit of $14,000.

"I was excited," Shook said of the first year's return. "Finally, I had a company that made a profit."

In that same year, Shook met George Haney, a skilled technician who helped build whatever units Shook sold.

"He was very headstrong and stubborn about the way things were built," Shook said. "He and I clashed constantly."

Though the combination was volatile at times, Shook and Haney made a great team. As the company grew, they began to find new applications for the 10,000-psi pumps.

"I began to call on automotive assembly plants, where we discovered great applications in the painting area," Shook said. "We began removing paint over spray from floor grates, paint booth back sections and exhaust stacks."

National Liquid Blasting developed a product called SPIN JET® and got a patent on the product to remove paint buildup from floor grates. According to Shook, the device saved car companies millions of dollars per year in labor and chemicals.

"Another big area of growth was in getting people interested in becoming cleaning contractors," Shook said. "A lot of the plants I was calling on wanted people to come in and do the work for them. We began to help get people started in the contract cleaning business. They would buy portable pumps from NLB and go into the plants to do the work."

In 1991, Shook was named Manufacturer/Entrepreneur of the Year by his industry peers in the state of Michigan.

The true turning point came when Shook and his team began to find applications within the chemical, petrochemical, power generation and pulp and paper industries.

"A key challenge was to develop pumps that could withstand ever-higher pressures," Shook said. "In the beginning we couldn't find pumps in the United States that would hold up to high-pressure cleaning applications without cracking in the fluid end. It was also a challenge to develop packing seals that would last for 1,000 hours instead of 40, 50 or 100 hours."

Such challenges seem small compared to those Shook faced during his days at the dump. The most important lesson he learned along the way to becoming successful, however, was that the development of quality equipment and a commitment to customer service are vital to a company's survival.

"I found out a long time ago that if you can't build quality products and fulfill the needs of your customers, you will not be successful," Shook said. "The key for us early on was to understand our customers' needs and the problems they had to solve. Once we had a better understanding of the problems, we were able to adapt high-pressure water to

138

solve them."

NLB soon branched out into surface prep, which could be performed at almost any type of plant.

"The growth that was occurring at NLB was exciting to say the least," Shook said. "The more we learned about waterjetting applications, the more we found out about the business as a whole. Watching the company grow has always given me a great feeling because it indicates the size of the market and the potential for future growth."

As NLB began to tackle tougher jobs, it built more pumps at higher pressures and expanded its personnel, plant and inventory.

The business continued to grow through the years — branch offices were opened in Texas, Louisiana, New Jersey and California, and NLB became a trusted name in the waterjetting equipment industry. In 1991, Shook was named Manufacturer/Entrepreneur of the Year by his industry peers in the state of Michigan. Since then, Shook has watched his company expand at the national and international levels. The company recently celebrated its 35th anniversary, and although NLB is as strong as it has ever been, the story is far from over.

NLB Corp. is a leading manufacturer of high-pressure and ultrahigh-pressure waterjetting equipment up to 40,000 psi. Its product line includes the 10,000-24,000 psi 225 series convertible pump.

"Believe it or not, we are still finding new applications for waterjetting equipment," Shook said. "We are growing faster now than at any time in our history."

* * *

According to Shook, the key to sustaining success over a long period of time is to foster a steady environment of interaction, both within the company and outside of it.

"We continue to work hard to make [NLB] a strong team environment with good communication for internal and external customers," he said.

In his spare time, Shook enjoys playing golf and boating on the Great Lakes. He often spends time sharing in the interests of his sons, Brian and Jeff. Brian is a trainer of show horses and Jeff, who works for NLB, is involved in the restoration of lighthouses along the Great Lakes.

Inside the office, Shook has set a standard for people inside and outside of his organization to follow.

"Work, work, work, and the harder you work, the luckier you are," he said. "Know what is needed by your customers."

In a relatively short period of time, Forrest Shook went from living to survive day-by-day to securing a prosperous future for himself, his family and his employees. Through hard work and creativity, Shook changed the minds of people who didn't believe that he could fulfill his dreams of success.

Despite his many achievements, Shook refuses to give himself all the credit. Rather than pointing out a single person who has inspired him to achieve excellence over the years, Shook always commends the many people who have made NLB's success possible when discussing the company's evolution. Perhaps his humble beginnings left such an indelible impression on him that he can't help but keep things in perspective.

"My heroes are the NLB employees. They are the ones who make things happen, and they do a great job," Shook said.

DAVID
STARKEY
CEO
Empire Scaffold

David Starkey has never been afraid to step outside his comfort zone. If he had, he would still be successful, but perhaps not on such a large scale.

Starkey, a native of Central, La., is the president and CEO of Empire Scaffold, an independent scaffolding company that offers rental, erection and dismantling services to the petrochemical and pulp and paper industries. Empire Scaffold, according to Starkey, represents the latest phase in a career built on courage and teamwork.

As an up-and-coming executive for the industrial scaffolding division of Hullinghorst Industries in the early '80s, Starkey led an effort to introduce a product manufactured by Scaffold Great Britain (SGB) that revolutionized the industrial scaffolding industry in the United States.

"We looked at a system scaffold called SGB Cuplok," Starkey said. "It was a modular type system scaffold. Prior to that most industrial scaffold was erected out of a steel scaffold referred to as 'tube and clamp,' which was about 40 percent slower to erect. Cuplok was here in the United States as a shoring scaffold, but we tried to bring it to the petrochemical industry."

Starkey discovered this system scaffolding after conceiving an idea to make assembly easier and quicker. He explained the idea to an engineer who later found that system scaffolding, which was highly similar in practice to Starkey's idea, was being used in a shoring capacity at a Crown Zellerbach site in St. Francisville, La.

"He called me and told me that the system scaffolding was doing exactly what I was talking about," Starkey said. "We went out to look at it, and there it was. SGB only made a few sizes, so we met with them and said we'd use it if they'd make more sizes. They had no previous intent to use it in an industrial setting."

Starkey and his partners had stumbled across an idea they felt could change the way scaffolding was assembled at industrial sites. Getting the industry to buy in, however, would prove to be a difficult task. To say that the group was ridiculed is an understatement, according to Starkey.

"I was brand new compared to some of the people in the industry at that time," Starkey said. "We took a lot of abuse. I was told on more than one occasion that I was nothing more than a tractor salesman and that I didn't know what I was doing. Even my partner's bank and trust department wondered if I had lost my mind."

Undeterred, Starkey and his team began using the system scaffold everywhere they worked. Today, the numerous types of system scaffolding are standard in the petrochemical, power, offshore, and pulp and paper industries.

"It changed the whole industry in the United States," Starkey said. "At the time I didn't know any better. A lot of the older foremen refused to put up the system scaffolding, so I had to hire younger foremen and get them calculators and clipboards in order to show them how to set it up. Once they caught on, the older guys said, 'Well, we'd better learn how to use this.'

"We introduced the first new product in the scaffolding industry, and there haven't been many changes since then," he added.

The feat resulted in SGB's purchase of the company led by Starkey and his partners, who would strengthen the scaffolding giant's foothold in the United States.

"They manufactured what we needed and supported us, and it worked out well," he said.

This coup of sorts set the tone for the careers of Starkey and his partners. What the group lacked in credibility early on, they made up for in tenacity. Of course, their success would not have been possible without hard work and dedication.

Raised on a farm in Central, Starkey learned early in life the value of hard work.

"My dad was a superintendent for the post office, but he'd go in at five o'clock in the mornings and get home early in the afternoons, so he worked on the farm," Starkey said. "We raised cattle, hogs, chicken, horses — just about everything except goats. I was expected to work five-and-a-half days a week when not in school — I always got off at noon on Saturdays. My mother was a school teacher, so she always pushed me to study hard and make good grades."

When asked how he feels about having spent his formative years doing manual labor in the unforgiving heat of the Louisiana sun, Starkey's response is telling.

"It was fun," he said. "I enjoyed it."

His time spent on the family farm helped Starkey in his career as a farm equipment salesman for Breeden Tractor. Starkey held that job until he was 30 years old, when he encountered a customer who would forever change the course of his professional life — Armand Hullinghorst, owner of Hullinghorst Industries.

"Mr. Hullinghorst didn't have an agricultural background," Starkey said. "I got to know him by helping him with his farm equipment."

Impressed by Starkey's knowledge and work ethic, Hullinghorst began making overtures to the young salesman to join his company as its first full-time scaffolding yard manager. Soon enough, Starkey joined Hullinghorst Industries and moved quickly up the ranks from manager of material shipping to general manager of the company and, eventually, executive vice president.

Five years after being hired by Hullinghorst, however, a pivotal and tragic event left Starkey at a crossroads.

"Unexpectedly, [Mr. Hullinghorst] was diagnosed with cancer," Starkey said. "He died 100 days after he found out."

Hullinghorst bequeathed 95 percent of his company to a trust for his family — the other five percent went to Starkey, who was named president of the company.

"I was thinking about getting out of the contracting business when all that happened, but he tied me down to it," Starkey said. "I had been selling products, and so I probably would have gone back into sales because I liked it."

A mentality of brotherhood has allowed David Starkey and his partners to compete successfully in the unique and competitive scaffolding industry.

Starkey, however, chose to accept the great responsibility thrust upon him, accumulating a wealth of knowledge about business along the way.

"At the time Mr. Hullinghorst died, I didn't have a lot of knowledge of business," Starkey said. "I hadn't even seen a financial statement. But he had faith in me."

Hullinghorst's faith in Starkey kept the latter believing he could succeed after his mentor's death.

Shortly after he took over Hullinghorst Industries, the company's scaffolding division was bought out by another man Starkey considers a mentor, Tom Branton. Branton orchestrated the sale of that division to SGB in 1987 after its success with SGB Cuplok.

"We worked for SGB and we thought everybody would retire there, be happy and live their lives," Starkey said. "Neil Woods, who was the CEO of SGB, taught us a lot about the scaffold business. But SGB did some things with their money in the United Kingdom that were not wise. They built an airport in downtown London and almost went broke doing it, so they sold the U.S. division to Brand."

The sale of the scaffolding division meant that up to 75 percent of its U.S. employees would lose their jobs. Starkey and 13 other partners out of what was known as the Southeast region responded by pulling together and forming a brand new company — United Scaffolding. Starkey and his partners operated United Scaffolding for a full decade before equity investors owned more stock than the founders. An unsuccessful attempt to repurchase United Scaffolding led Starkey and five of his partners to strike out on their own.

"We looked for a small scaffolding company to buy and we found

144

a company in Monroe, La., that had a good team, so we bought it," he said.

That small, team-oriented company was Empire Scaffold. The purchase was finalized in September 2002. As of 2007, Starkey and his partners had grown the company tenfold and opened locations in Houston and Beaumont, Texas, in addition to its corporate office in Baton Rouge, La.

* * *

Empire Scaffold's ownership team now includes seven partners — Starkey, Robert Kusch, Ernie Sanders, Clarence Cheatham, Tommy Graham, Coy Smith and Jerry Sylvester, who led the company before its purchase — and a couple of silent partners. The group includes men who have worked closely together for two to three decades. Although the

> *"Being involved in so many startups, I've seen lots of things. You really find out who your friends are. God is always your friend. The relationship you have with God and your faith and determination are part of any business."*

opportunities for growth are there for the taking, the team is satisfied with the company's standing. Furthermore, Starkey is a firm believer in working within the means of his organization.

"We can grow it very quickly, but we have to be sure we don't grow ourselves to death," Starkey said. "We won't take on a project we don't think we can handle. When we take on something very big, however, it doesn't scare us. As a matter of fact, this team has done some of the biggest scaffold jobs in the United States."

Starkey feels that his company's strong focus on its specialty and its relatively small size — its payroll averages 375 at any given time — work in tandem to keep quality, customer service and employee relations at high levels.

"Some companies try to be everything to everyone, but we're not interested in that," Starkey said. "We are a scaffolding company. We specialize in anything from offshore rig work, paper mills, power plants, chemical plants and refineries, but we're not one of the big boys. However, if someone's looking for cheap work, they had better get it somewhere else. We don't compete with cheap — we make quality affordable.

"Our strength is that we're not so big that we don't know our own people," he said. "It's happened to us in previous companies where we didn't know our own superintendents. We know our superintendents here. And when a customer calls here, there's a good chance he'll be able to speak to an owner. Furthermore, we've always believed that if you go to the dance with us, we're going to take you home. We stick to our customers through thick and thin. We've had some get into trouble, but we've worked with them."

Empire Scaffold's success was made possible and is maintained by its team of experienced and hard-working individuals.

"It takes a unique person to be in this industry," Starkey said. "You have to be a flexible and determined individual — it's a lot of hard work. I look for people that are educated in the industry, but can also be taught. I also look for people with honesty and integrity. My partners and I don't believe in ill-gotten gains. We're all Christians, and there are two deacons among us."

The company's mentality of brotherhood has allowed it to compete successfully in a unique and competitive industry.

David Starkey, left, is shown here with his partners in the Empire Scaffold corporate office in Baton Rouge, La. — Coy Smith, second from left, Robert Kusch, second from right, and Tommy Graham.

"We're all competitors, but we're also friends," he said. "We don't try to beat anyone out of anything. If I need something, they're going to charge me for it, and vice versa, but we're also going to help each other out. We don't want to take anything that's not there for us."

Honesty, integrity and teamwork are at the top of the list when you consider the keys to success in any business. Starkey, however, urges budding entrepreneurs to place as much emphasis on finances as they do on values.

Empire Scaffold's Houston office is led by, from left, Clarence Cheatham and Ernest Sanders.

"I think one of the greatest things I've learned is the importance of budgeting and scheduling," Starkey said. "I was surprised to learn from people in the financial business that we're one of the few companies of our size that does budgets and projections. You can build a lot of scaffolding and do a great job, but if you don't watch the financial side, it'll get you into a lot of trouble. No one should go into any business without a budget. If it doesn't work on paper, it won't work in real time."

From Starkey's vantage point, Empire Scaffold's path to continued prosperity has been carved. Further expansion, however, is a question of will.

"It all depends on how badly the owners want to grow," Starkey said. "We can probably double our size in three or four more years depending on how much capital we invest."

In the meantime, Starkey intends to further his company's commitment to quality on the job while retaining an occupation that gives him respite during downtime. Starkey, along with his wife Jerry, still lives on the farm in Central where he developed his work ethic. Although there aren't any animals (except for one horse) left to tend to, there is still plenty of work to be done on the property — the Starkeys are now tree farmers. Aside from doing farm work, they enjoy spending their leisure time with their three children and nine grandchildren, who range in age from six months to 22 years.

Starkey begins each day at the office knowing things will eventually be OK because of the support of good friends on Earth and beyond.

"Being involved in so many startups, I've seen lots of things," he said. "You really find out who your friends are. God is always your friend. The relationship you have with God and your faith and determination are part of any business. All of my partners feel the same way. I can't do this

147

by myself, and they can't do it by themselves."

Determination, tenacity, faith, teamwork and smart management. Most successful entrepreneurs would agree that these are the keys to making dreams come true. David Starkey and his partners are living proof.

BERT
TURNER
Chairman Emeritus
Turner Industries

In December 2000, Turner Industries founder Bert S. Turner sat down in front of a video camera in his Baton Rouge, La., home and answered questions about his life asked by Sari Turner, the wife of his son Thomas. Then 79 years of age, Turner told stories of his childhood in small sawmill towns in Louisiana and Missouri; his maturation as a student of the LSU engineering school; his service in the Army Corps of Engineers during World War II; his courtship of his wife; his rapid rise as an employee of Esso and Nichols Construction Inc.; and the founding of Turner Industries.

His account paints a picture of a life filled with love, stress, happiness, hard work, heartache, humility and dreams, nearly all of which were fulfilled. The video only clocks in at an hour and 45 minutes — surely there is much to the story that will be preserved only in casual recollections by Bert and by his family, friends and colleagues. Still, the videotaped conversation captures the highlights of a great American success story, the tale of a man who rose from poverty to become one of the most revered industrial construction entrepreneurs of his generation.

What stands out most, however, is the final statement, prompted by a request from Sari to send a message to future generations of his family.

At first, he appears apprehensive. He expresses his concern that any advice given by him to people living in an entirely different world will be obsolete. Indeed, the world of 2000 was vastly different from that which he knew as a young adult — he served in the military during America's defining moment as a world superpower and worked for Exxon when it was still known as Esso — so one can only imagine what the lives of his descendents in, say, 2050 will be like.

But after a moment of deliberation he takes a deep breath and begins to share a very simple philosophy sure to resonate throughout the ages. It's about the importance of self-analysis and reflection.

"We probably all need to stop and take time to ask ourselves the questions that you've asked me," he told his daughter-in-law. "Because I think we're in a rush to do the things we do, and we think they're important, but when we back off and analyze them, we see that they really are not. We should do a better job of trying to prioritize what we're going to do and the way we're going to do it."

Bert grins, and the screen fades to black. The viewer immediately begins to internalize these words of wisdom because he or she knows that many of us won't be fortunate enough to engage in things we're passionate about when we're 85, as does Bert. Even though it's been more than a decade since he named 30-year Turner veteran Roland Toups chairman and CEO and Thomas chief operating officer (effectively relinquishing most of his responsibilities as an executive), Bert still makes daily visits to the company's Baton Rouge headquarters to keep an eye on things.

Each day he sits behind his desk, Bert is standing on the advice he shared with the world of the future, taking inventory and making sure that the top priorities of his company, and thus, his family, are being handled in a way that will keep Turner Industries growing in the new century.

* * *

Bert Silger Turner was born in 1921 in Elizabeth, La., to Grover Cleveland Turner and Margaret Ann Silger Turner. Throughout his childhood, Bert and his parents lived in sawmill towns as his hardworking father traveled to various places installing mills and producing lumber.

When Bert was just eight years old, Grover drowned while fishing near the home of his wife's relatives. Losing his father at such a young age could have easily hindered his development. Margaret, however, did everything she could to ensure her son would grow up to be the kind of man who could provide for himself and a family. This was especially chal-

150

lenging as it had to be done during one of the darkest periods in America's history.

"[The Great Depression] gave me a sense of value that I wouldn't have had otherwise," Bert said. "I also learned a lot of what it takes to accumulate wealth, which is a lot of hard work. There's also the element of being in the right place at the right time."

Bert and his mother moved from Louisiana to Margaret's hometown, Grandin, Mo., shortly after Grover's death. Margaret earned a living as a schoolteacher to provide for her son, and Bert found ways to raise money on his own.

Just three and a half years after beginning his studies, Bert Turner earned a bachelor's degree from Louisiana State University. Though his time at LSU was brief, he has always looked upon that period as his coming of age.

"We were about as poor as you could get," Bert said. "After my father's death, my mother's monthly salary was $60. I trapped rabbits, skinned them and got a dime apiece for them."

Bert's fondest memories of his time in Grandin include summers spent fishing and swimming with friends and snowy winters. After Bert graduated from high school, his mother made the decision to move herself and her son to Baton Rouge so that he could attend LSU, which boasted a top-notch engineering program.

Ironically, Bert earned his scholarship not because of his excellent marks in high school, but because there was a need for a baritone bugle player in LSU's Drum and Bugle Corps, which was part of the school's ROTC program. (Bert had tried previously to earn a music scholarship as a trombone player, but was unsuccessful.) Bert initially enrolled in LSU's chemical engineering department, but changed course shortly afterward.

"After my first semester, I decided I didn't like chemistry," Bert said. "I made an A in it, but it didn't excite me at all, so I swapped over to mechanical engineering. That didn't excite me a whole heck of a lot more, but it was much better than chemical engineering."

The transition would prove to be pivotal. Bert is certain that his life would have been very different had he not shifted gears.

"You really need to do something you know you're going to enjoy," Bert said. "If you don't like what you do, you're never going to do a very good job. In the business area, you've got to find out where you're happy. If you're happy, you'll probably succeed."

Just three and a half years after beginning his studies, Bert earned his bachelor's degree in mechanical engineering. Though his time at LSU was brief, he has always looked upon that period as his coming of age. As a member of the fraternity Delta Kappa Epsilon, he established long-lasting friendships and met Sue Wilbert, the woman with whom he'd spend the rest of his life. His involvement in the campus military program culminated with his appointment as cadet colonel for the ROTC engineers, a key development in his evolution as a leader. Bert also worked 24 hours per week while attending school, binding and repairing books and proofreading theses and dissertations for LSU's bindery. In addition, he learned to fly an airplane and served as president of the College of Engineering.

After college, Bert went to Fort Belvoir in Virginia and obtained the equivalent of ROTC Summer Camp. He was then commissioned as a second lieutenant in the Army Corps of Engineers and served in a battalion that was attached to the Air Force in the Pacific during World War II. His time at war was mostly free of danger — the battalion with which he

Turner, right, first went into business for himself in 1961, founding a new industrial construction firm called Nichols Construction Corp. after resigning from Yuba Consolidated Industries. He is pictured here with Rainer Moeller of Demag North America.

served was only fired upon once, though three of Bert's closest friends were killed in other battles. After the surrenders of the Axis forces in the Pacific and in Europe, Bert spent six months commanding a battalion that built or rebuilt barracks, hospitals and roads in Japan for civilians and troops.

In 1946, Bert returned to Baton Rouge and approached his former professors at LSU to inquire about job opportunities. George Matthes, head of the mechanical engineering department, recommended that he pursue employment with Esso and arranged for Bert to meet three of the company's department heads. Soon after, he was

152

offered a job, and went to work for the company as a process control engineer. Fifteen months into his employment, Bert applied to Esso's educational foundation and obtained a scholarship to Harvard Business School. Bert and Sue moved to Boston shortly after they were married and lived there until Bert earned his MBA.

Bert returned to Esso in Baton Rouge and worked on a number of projects in various departments. During that time, he met Bob Nichols, president of Nichols Construction Co. Inc., and later went on to work for him as an assistant. Just 15 months after Bert was hired, Nichols died of an intestinal disease, leaving his widow to decide the future of the compa-

> *"You really need to do something you know you're going to enjoy. If you don't like what you do, you're never going to do a very good job. In the business area, you've got to find out where you're happy. If you're happy, you'll probably succeed."*

ny. Nichols Construction was sold to Yuba Consolidated Industries of California in 1959. Bert was named vice president and general manager of Nichols Construction, which became a division of Yuba.

By 1961, Yuba was experiencing financial setbacks, and it later declared bankruptcy. It was at this time that Bert first went into business for himself, founding a new industrial construction firm called Nichols Construction Corp. after resigning from Yuba. (Bert and his partners used the Nichols name because of its high recognition within the industry.) Bert used the contacts he'd made in industry while working for Nichols Construction Co. Inc. and Yuba to grow the new business, which was an immediate success.

More than 40 years later, Turner Industries is a multifaceted industrial construction and maintenance and specialty services company with locations throughout the Gulf South. It prides itself on delivering quality service to industry with a commitment to safety and efficiency.

* * *

It's been almost five decades since Thomas Turner's father built the foundation of the empire atop which he and the other members of the Turner Industries management team now sit. Bert's success ensured that his five children — sons Thomas, John and Robert and daughters Susan and Mary — never had to endure the hardships their father experienced as a boy growing up during the Depression. Thomas, however, has seen his share of adversity.

After earning a bachelor's degree in general studies from LSU and an MBA from Tulane University, Thomas jumped right into the family business, unlike his siblings, each of whom went on to be successful in other careers. He joined Harmony, an open-shop contracting business owned by Turner, in 1980.

In 1982, Turner entered the waste disposal business by creating a new division called Acadian Waste, which was to be a direct competitor to Browning-Ferris Industries (BFI).

"We didn't know anything about the garbage business, so it floundered," Thomas said. "After about six months of that, my father asked me if I'd move over into it and try to figure out what needed to be done. I said, 'Absolutely not. I don't know why we're even in such a stinky business.'"

Despite his son's apprehensions, Bert was able to convince Thomas to hold his nose and attempt to solve the problems hindering Acadian Waste. Thomas went full speed ahead, becoming directly involved in business development, marketing and finance. The six years he spent with Acadian Waste are still among the most stressful of his career to this date, but in that time the company became Louisiana's largest private waste hauler. In 1988, Acadian Waste was purchased by BFI, and Thomas went along with it. He handled acquisitions for BFI for about a year, but returned to Turner Industries after his contract expired.

At that time, Turner Industries had begun to dabble in the environmental remediation business. When Thomas returned to the company, he

154

became part of a new environmental remediation division that sputtered many times before eventually turning the corner — it now thrives under the umbrella of Turner Specialty Services. Thomas also revamped Turner Industries' human resources department by instituting risk management corporate safety programs.

Thomas Turner first joined Turner Industries in 1980, and now serves as chief operating officer.

According to Thomas, beginning his career with Turner in the mid- to late-'80s, when the oil and gas industry along the Gulf Coast was at its nadir, was a trial by fire.

"I grew up in this business, so I got to see the good, the bad and the ugly," Thomas said. "I got to live through a period in the '80s when we had to fire thousands of people. That was extremely difficult. Things were tough here, but fortunately we were one of the very few contractors in the region that didn't lose money. Many of the others went out of business."

Thomas learned under harsh circumstances the importance of treating people with dignity.

"Through the course of all that I was exposed to the business ethic of treating people firmly but fairly," Thomas said. "Employee relations were totally different back then, but I learned that honesty is the best policy."

The people-first mentality has carried on throughout the years. This becomes evident as Thomas recalls a pivotal moment in the history of Turner Industries — a deal that could have benefited his family immensely. About six years ago, the Turner management team had the opportunity to sell the company to a local competitor.

"During the course of the negotiations, our management team came together and agreed that we couldn't get a feel for what would happen to our employees if we sold," Thomas said. "We decided that unless we were sure about that, we'd walk away from the table."

The Turner family rejected the other company's offer, setting the stage for a culture of loyalty between employees and management that is stronger now than it's ever been before.

"What made it so memorable was the fact that everybody rallied

155

together," Thomas said. "I think that has accelerated our growth because it put everybody absolutely on the same page. I think that our employees saw our commitment to them, and so it turned around and it has been very beneficial."

The company's team mentality has been crucial in recent times, as the Gulf Coast hurricanes of 2005 challenged industry and its service providers in many ways.

"Many of our employees went through a lot of personal heartache, but they really rallied because at the same time they knew that they had to get the job done to get the plants back in operation," Thomas said. "This year's been absolutely crazy. We've worked more man hours than we ever have before, and it's been under a lot of mental stress."

Thomas expresses much pride in the perseverance of his people. Having experienced a number of challenges early in his own career, he expects nothing less. Fortunately, the company's competitiveness has remained stable due to the legacy of smart management that has been passed like a torch from Bert to Roland Toups, Thomas and the rest of the executive team (Don McCollister, Billy Guitreau, Dave Lauve and Bob Pearson run the company's construction, maintenance, equipment and specialty services, and fabrication divisions, respectively).

"One of the things that always acted as a safety net for the company was that early on, my father — along with the other guys he worked with — recognized the importance of having maintenance contracts," Thomas said. "So even in those really lean years, the ongoing maintenance work always paid the bills. That helped us through the hard times. In addition to that, we always tried to do everything we could to embrace technology, and I think that helped us quite a bit."

Perhaps more than anything, Bert has instilled within his protégés a work ethic and a commitment to responsible leadership one would expect from a man who has truly earned everything the future generations of his family and his company can call their own.

"If you really want to accomplish an objective, you've got to work hard at it, in many different ways," Bert said in his 2000 interview. "And I learn more and more all the time that relationships with people are important. You have to be straightforward, but also put yourself in the

156

other person's shoes more frequently than most of us do before making a decision. You don't have to be a softy, but I think sometimes we make decisions before we really have thought about the impact they might have on others."

* * *

Bert has made a tremendous impact on countless people. He and Sue have donated significant amounts of time and money to many community organizations and educational institutions — including the United Way and LSU — through the years. The current management team of Turner Industries will do the same for as long as the company remains under its leadership.

Bert's impact is hard to quantify, and the number of great stories that make up the volumes of Turner lore will never be counted. However, there is one of which Thomas is particularly fond, and it's conspicuously absent from the 2000 interview.

In the early '70s, Bert purchased a luxury automobile with an engine made for a police car. One day, he drove it to Plaquemine, La., to submit a bid to a Georgia-Pacific plant (now Georgia Gulf) that was due at noon.

"On the way to the plant, the car started to overheat," Thomas said. "Well, the bid had to be in at noon — not a minute later — and so he kept driving."

Bert arrived at the plant in time to submit the bid. Just a few minutes afterward, however, he heard sirens. Bert walked outside to the plant's parking lot to find that his new car had gone up in flames — the sirens were emanating from a plant fire truck that had been dispatched to fight the blaze.

Although he lost his prized automobile and had to drive home in a company pickup truck, Nichols Construction won its first significantly large job from an industrial plant. It was the job that put Nichols on the map, and the story of how it came to be is a great encapsulation of what has made Bert Turner and Turner Industries successful — the timeless qualities of determination and sound judgment in the face of adversity.

VERMILLION

Owners
Glove Guard L.P.

Many wedded couples say that a marriage is a lot like a business partnership. When two people marry, they enter a contract whereupon they will work together to build and maintain a functioning household. They agree to share in making decisions about everything related to a home, children, transportation, finances and the myriad other issues families face on a daily basis.

In order for the partnership to thrive, each person must make an effort to fulfill his or her role. If responsibilities within the household and at work are not balanced, one will fall by the wayside and affect the other in a detrimental way. Roles must be clearly defined, but neither partner should be reluctant to step outside his or her comfort zone when necessary.

It's no wonder that many married couples who go into business together succeed both personally and professionally. As their personal relationships mature, they acquire skills that allow them to function better in the workplace. Of course, not all married couples succeed in business together, and the reasons are naturally more complicated than any sets of circumstances that cause ordinary professional partnerships to fail. When the chemistry's right, however, two people can share a vision for their lives and do whatever is necessary to see it through.

Kenneth and Shelia Vermillion of Highlands, Texas, went into business together more than seven years ago and have experienced more personal and professional satisfaction than they ever did before. They purchased Glove Guard — a manufacturer of belt-loop clips for protective gloves used in industry and other settings — in 1999 on a leap of faith, and have worked hand-in-hand to grow it ever since. The company now manufactures the Glove Guard®, the patent-pending Utility Guard™ — a modified version of the Glove Guard that attaches directly to belts — and the Utility Bag™. Each of the products has a patented breakaway system that prevents personnel from being pulled into machinery or losing their balance when gloves get snagged on nearby objects.

It wasn't the Vermillions' first business partnership. They had considered everything from chicken farms to car washes in the past, but had yet to find the venture that best fit their interests and capabilities. Shelia, meanwhile, had begun a business venture of her own, providing bookkeeping and tax services at home.

"As a wife and mother, it was my desire to be at home with Kenneth and our two sons — Bryan and Bradley — and work to produce supplemental income for vacations," Shelia said. "A home-based business was the only viable solution, and since I loved to use my accounting skills, a bookkeeping and tax business was the natural choice."

One of her customers was Jo Ellen Coker, owner of Go Finder Services Inc. and inventor of the original Glove Guard.

"When Jo Ellen first came to me for bookkeeping services, Kenneth encouraged me to accept the challenge," Shelia said. "Eventually, she asked me to provide packaging, shipping and warehousing services for her growing business."

Kenneth, who worked for 25 years as a journeyman electrician and three years in the telecommunications business, saw the potential of Glove Guard in the industrial marketplace and encouraged Shelia to help Coker grow Glove Guard by hiring her own staff. By the time Coker was ready to sell the business, the Vermillions knew that they could manage it themselves and maintain its success.

"Neither of us was afraid of hard work or failure," Shelia said. "We both wanted a business that would allow us some freedom and flexibility in our work week. Also, it has always been our dream to meet and visit people in every state in the U.S. We realized those things could only be accomplished by establishing a team of like-minded people. Therefore, we purposefully stepped out to build a business on the concept of people

160

helping people."

* * *

Before they could help other people, however, they sought guidance from above, relying on their faith to overcome the challenges of taking over the fledgling business.

"We had three very big challenges to overcome — financing, the legality of business and patents, and the issues husbands and wives working together must face," Shelia said. "Superficially, the financing side of the equation was the most overwhelming issue. For us, however, it was the easiest part to rest in. We made it a matter of what you might call reverse prayer: 'Lord, don't let the financing happen if it's not Your will for us to have this business.' We knew by experiential faith that God gives best to those who leave the choice to Him. The only way the funds would come available would be through His intervention. Of course, we also knew that the best does not always mean that everything is going to be rosy. We knew there would be plenty of thorns to deal with."

As it turned out, the Vermillions were able to secure the financing. Then came the fun part — ironing out the legal issues of establishing a business in which patents are involved.

"That may not sound like a big deal to some, but it was to us," Shelia said. "We had never spoken to lawyers — besides an uncle who happened to be in the profession — but we suddenly found ourselves meeting with three per day. The old saying, 'You don't know you have a problem until you talk to a lawyer,' is true, but we found those interactions to be very helpful. We also learned that the money spent for sound legal advice and a professional CPA is well worth it."

Seeking expert advice is an essential component when taking over a business. Although the business owner is responsible for making final decisions, the information he or she gleans from lawyers, accountants and business consultants should not be ignored, Shelia said.

The framework for the Vermillions' working relationship was modeled on that of their marriage. Shelia trusted Kenneth to make the most important decisions, even though they were always informed by her

161

perspectives and insights.

"The idea of Kenneth and I working together 24/7 seemed exhausting," Shelia said. "It was then and still is, but that's what life is all about — working and getting along with people, including your spouse."

They always got along as husband and wife, but Shelia admits to being apprehensive about how business matters would affect that relationship, and vice versa.

"At first it was very difficult to carry on business discussions without letting our personal feelings and frustrations flow into the decision-making process," Shelia said. "We find it extremely important to separate business from personal feelings in any working relationship, especially if the partners are married. What worked for me was a concept I learned in accounting — put everything in black and white."

Shelia's ability to simplify business decisions by looking through a monochromatic mental lens resulted in a creative practice that has all but eliminated the emotional element in the Vermillions' working relationship.

"Anytime it became apparent in business meetings that a clear separation needed to be made, I would take a piece of paper, and write 'wife' on one side and 'business partner' on the other," Shelia said. "The side that needed to be represented would face upward. For us, this one little piece of paper helped separate our thought processes, and it accomplished the important task of keeping us both on the same page."

Once they were able to draw the line between their marriage and their business partnership, they truly became a team both inside the office and at home. This achievement, in turn, helped them to progress as managers and trust their employees to work with them in fulfilling their vision.

"Part of being a good leader is to allow others to step out on their own, make plans and execute," Shelia said. "We have found the illustration given in the Bible of how a body of believers should operate as an excellent example of how teamwork within a business should operate. We believe a business should function on the basis that everyone has an important role within the organization. We all have different strengths and weaknesses, and our goal is to operate within the areas of their strengths.

We have been fortunate to find many employees and associates who share our values and work ethics."

Among the aforementioned values is integrity, a virtue the Vermillions have taken seriously ever since they've been in business. They've held strong to their commitment to manufacturing quality products and have maintained excellent relations with their customers and distributors.

"We've had the opportunity to become friends with many of our distributors across the United States and abroad," Shelia said. "Vision Safe — our wholesale distributor in Australia — is owned by a couple named

> *"Failure is not the big issue when you're in business. It's how you deal with adverse situations that results in true success."*
>
> — Shelia Vermillion

Dean and Jenni Roberts. We've become well acquainted with them because we face the same challenges, even though we operate businesses on opposite sides of the world. It's nice to have mutual respect and friendship among people as part of business relationships. That's the most rewarding part to me, and it's my measure of success."

A measure of success that's had a more profound effect on Glove Guard's bottom line is the reputation the company has gained for enhancing personnel safety in industry. Glove Guard has prevented hand injuries by up to 86 percent, and many companies have mandated use of the product in their safety programs. Customers have found the Utility Bag — which comes in different varieties, including open-mesh bags for tools and pouches for eyeglasses and goggles — to be useful in keeping valuable items close at hand without compromising safety.

* * *

From left, Bryan, Ken, Shelia and Bradley Vermillion work together at the Glove Guard office. Ken and Shelia have provided their sons with a lifelong clinic on teamwork and entrepreneurship.

In the past two years, Bryan and Bradley Vermillion have become full-time Glove Guard employees. One can only imagine what issues arose from that. According to Shelia, however, the family of four has always worked as a team, making the parents' task of bringing their two sons into the fold relatively easy.

"The boys always had an idea of what it would be like to work with Mom and Dad," Shelia said. "They have taken part in the complete construction of one of our homes and our first warehouse. The full construction of the warehouse, as a matter of fact, was done almost completely by Kenneth, Bryan and Bradley. Kenneth will tackle almost any job, and the two boys have learned that when Dad says he has a project and he'd like them to help, they had better get ready to work."

The boys also had a hand in constructing Glove Guard's new office and warehouse space, which was completed in October 2006.

The team concept carries over to the family's leisure activities as well.

"We enjoy the outdoors, and we hunt together as a family," Shelia said. "The boys grew up going out to a deer stand with me, and when they became old enough, they graduated to hunting with their dad. Hunting set the stage for a lot of ethics and values that both boys carried with them into adulthood."

When the family returns home from their hunts, they form an assembly line on which they clean game and package meat for meals. The Vermillions eat plenty of harvested venison, and they also make link sausage in their very own smokehouse.

"Our children grew up knowing that food did not come just from the grocery store," Shelia said. "When the boys were younger, we raised our own chickens. We would receive 50 heavy broiler chicks in March and prepare them on Memorial Day for packaging. Between that and the veni-

164

son, it provided most of the meat we would eat throughout the course of the year."

Bradley, who earned a bachelor's degree in electrical engineering from Texas A&M University in 2004, manages the company's warehouse, designs its graphics and performs research and design work. He worked part-time for the company during his junior high and high school years, so he was well prepared when he made the decision in 2005 to begin his career in the family business. Bryan received a mechanical engineering degree from Lamar University in Beaumont, Texas, and worked as an application engineer for a petrochemical pump manufacturer for five years before joining Glove Guard in 2006. He has since taken over office administration and is managing the company's international division and performing research and design work.

"Working together in business as a family has been a learning experience for all of us," Shelia said. "The working relationship is quite different than the family relationship of parents and children. The challenge for Kenneth and me is to refrain from looking at the two young men as our sons while they are learning to relate to us as co-workers instead of parents. All of us tend to look at things differently in the work environment as opposed to the home environment. The ethics and values remain the same in both arenas, but the perspective is very different."

The Vermillions' perspective on entrepreneurship has remained the same through the years. They do not allow the fear of failure to keep them apart from their dreams of success and satisfaction.

"Failure is not the big issue when you're in business," Shelia said. "It's how you deal with adverse situations that results in true success."

To illustrate her family's view on how much control one has over his or her own destiny, Shelia quoted the evangelical pastor Charles Swindoll, who said the following:

"The longer I live, the more I realize the impact of attitude on life. Attitude is more important than education, than money, than circumstances, than failures, than successes, than what other people think or say or do. The remarkable thing is we have a choice every day regarding the attitude we will embrace for that day. We cannot change the inevitable. The only thing we can do is play on the one string we have, and that is our attitude. I am convinced that life is 10 percent what happens to me and 90 percent how I react to it."

Faith and family have taken Kenneth and Shelia Vermillion a long way, and with their sons at their sides and a healthy perspective on their personal and professional lives, it seems as though the journey has only just begun.

"As partners in this business, Kenneth and I manage to balance each other in order to be both disciplined and flexible," Shelia said. "Our strongest attributes are the ones we have learned as husband and wife and then implemented in the business partnership. We know the best thing we can do is help each other succeed."

The Vermillions have provided their sons with a lifelong clinic on teamwork, ensuring the future success of the company they've worked so hard to grow.

"In the early years of the business, they would watch us and say that aliens had inhabited their parents' bodies," Shelia said. "Now we tell them they'd better watch out or they'll be acting strange as well. Entrepreneurship will do that to you."

PETE
VRETTAKOS
CEO & Chairman
Atlantic Industrial

Pete Vrettakos dreamed big during the early days of his career in the scaffolding industry. Given the architectural wonders located in the nation's capital, which lay just outside his then-employer's sphere of influence, it wasn't difficult to aim high.

Working as a scaffold erector for a Baltimore-based scaffolding company in his early 20s, Vrettakos took every chance he could to admire the historic buildings that line the streets of nearby Washington. Most of his time on the job, however, was spent scaling government buildings and churches in Baltimore and Annapolis, Md.

Eventually, Vrettakos was given the opportunity to participate in the renovation of the Old Post Office Clock Tower, a historic government building on Pennsylvania Avenue. The job included estimating, building and everything else in between. It was the most exciting and pivotal job of Vrettakos's career up to that point.

"Being young and ambitious, I went back to the management and expressed my desire to open a branch of the company there," Vrettakos said.

The company, however, was not interested in expanding to that area, so Vrettakos decided that in order to advance his career, he'd have to move on. Although he had no immediate backup plan, he was well connected. A man with whom he had previously worked in the industry — a sales manager for a well-known scaffolding rental and sales company in Washington — learned of Vrettakos's availability and promptly contacted him.

"He said that if I would set up a business and get licensed and insured, his company would give us leads of customers looking for professionals to do the work," Vrettakos said. "All we had to do was rent the scaffolding from his company.

"I really liked Washington," Vrettakos said. "I started picking out all the buildings I wanted to work on. One of them was the Willard Hotel on Pennsylvania Avenue and 14th Street, very close to the White House."

The Willard Hotel, which first opened in 1816, has hosted such political and cultural icons as Abraham Lincoln, Charles Dickens, Martin Luther King Jr., and Harry Houdini, among many others. Ulysses S. Grant held his inaugural party there, and Calvin Coolidge resided at the Willard for an entire month before taking office in 1923. The hotel closed in 1968, but was renovated in the early '80s. Vrettakos's work on that project opened his eyes to the wealth of opportunities in the D.C. area.

The partnership was an immediate success. Vrettakos's new company, Atlantic Rigging Corp., was contracted to provide rigging services to the United States Naval Observatory and the home of then-Vice President Walter Mondale, among other high profile government-related buildings.

Early on in his career, Pete Vrettakos was given the opportunity to participate in the renovation of the Old Post Office Clock Tower, a historic government building on Pennsylvania Avenue in Washington, D.C.

Vrettakos was rewarded sweetly for striking out on his own and working hard to achieve his dreams. Most entrepreneurs would agree that to leave a financially stable company and build a new business from the ground up is as risky as scaling the Washington Monument without a harness. Vrettakos, however, has courage and the spirit of the entrepreneur written into his DNA.

Vrettakos's father, who was born and raised in Greece, left his home country during World War II to live in America. Just 17 years of age at the time, he had a strong desire to fight alongside the Greek forces, who had been exiled from the country by the Axis powers. Rather than allowing their young son to become a guerrilla fighter, however, his

168

parents sent him to the United States, where he studied at the University of Virginia. After college, he went to work for Esso Standard Oil and eventually founded his own fuel oil delivery business.

"I learned my work ethic from him," Vrettakos said. "He worked very hard all his life."

It may very well be that his father's great American success story provided motivation on a subconscious level to help restore symbols of freedom. Attaining that goal, however, was just the first chapter in a success story that's far from over.

* * *

It took the kind of grit characteristic of a resistance fighter to grow the new business from a fledgling operation to the multifaceted service company it would become in the '90s.

"In the beginning there was never enough money, manpower or material," Vrettakos said. "I had no trouble getting the business. Washington needed a good scaffold construction company, as did much of the region. Resource shortages will probably never be totally overcome in my lifetime. But it did improve over time as we built a nucleus of quality employees and accumulated assets to leverage."

For the first few years, Atlantic Rigging made its mark by providing high-quality services to government and commercial entities. It wouldn't be long, however, before Vrettakos and company made their first foray into industry.

"In 1982 we got some opportunities with Baltimore Gas & Electric," Vrettakos said. "We did a big project scaffolding boilers in one of the power plants there for an asbestos abatement and insulation contractor. That was the beginning of our migration toward industrial markets."

Vrettakos and his team found industrial work to be a great fit because of Atlantic Rigging's focus on safety — a huge priority in all sectors of industry. In addition, Vrettakos found industrial managers easy to deal with when compared to commercial building contractors.

Atlantic's industrial work had begun in power generation, but later expanded into pulp and paper. For Vrettakos, however, the big prize was the petrochemical industry.

"I had heard from people I was exposed to at national conventions about the kind of work that was being done in the Gulf Coast petrochemical industry," Vrettakos said. "At the time our company had about 75 people working 10 or 15 jobs. I found it hard to believe that any scaffolding company had so many people working for them. But it was intriguing, and it became a target for me."

It would be another 15 years before Atlantic would begin to work in refineries. Even then, it was risky and expensive.

"We had hit a revenue plateau, and we just couldn't get over the hump," Vrettakos said. "We dominated the region we were in, but there really wasn't any refinery work to speak of."

In a déjà vu of sorts, Vrettakos received a phone call that would have a significant impact on the direction of his business. It was from a Brand Scaffolding employee who had experience working with the petrochemical industry and was interested in leaving his national business development director's position to work for Atlantic.

"So we had a meeting and decided to bring him on," Vrettakos said. "That was the first step toward getting into the petrochemical market. By that time we had opened a branch in Florida that was doing work in phosphate mines and power plants, so we had expanded geographically."

The company had finally tapped into the refinery business. However, the real turning point came in 1995 when Vrettakos discovered

Vrettakos's work on the historic Willard Hotel opened his eyes to the wealth of opportunities in the D.C. area.

a product that would secure his foothold in the industry — the Excel scaffold system, invented by scaffolding industry veteran and Louisiana native Joe Williams.

"I had always been a technology guy," Vrettakos said. "The reason why our business was successful was that we would design or invent tools to help us erect scaffolding."

In this particular case, the hard

work had already been done. Williams had created an automated locking scaffold system that boasted strength, durability, efficiency and safety. Vrettakos traveled to Louisiana to meet Williams and see his product first hand. He was immediately impressed.

"Joe invented the greatest scaffold system ever made," Vrettakos said. "We made a large purchase and put the system up in a Mobil Oil refinery in New Jersey. It was really difficult to get them to break from the scaffolding company they had been using."

As a matter of fact, the process was costly and its long-term effect on the profitability of Atlantic was uncertain.

"It is essential to be passionate about what you are doing. You need lots of drive to overcome the hurdles. And you don't have to be the smartest guy in the room, but you must be the most tenacious."

"I didn't know if it was going to break the company or be a big success," Vrettakos said.

Eventually, as Vrettakos forged a closer bond with Williams, the relationship with the refining industry grew stronger. In 1998, Williams's company merged into Atlantic.

"Joe was established in the refinery business throughout the country," Vrettakos said. "The different things each of us brought to the table were what really made Atlantic into the successful company it is today. We've become successful in a tightly knit, Gulf-Coast-centered industry. I wouldn't have thought that was possible 10 years ago."

According to Vrettakos, merging two companies based in different regions of the country was a challenge in and of itself. (Even though Maryland is south of the Mason-Dixon line, some people in the South consider Vrettakos and his mid-Atlantic colleagues to be Yankees.)

"I'm particularly proud of the fact that we were able to blend the two cultures — north and south — without having a civil war," Vrettakos said. "One of my biggest challenges was to create an environment where everyone could communicate and reach a common ground with regard to working philosophies."

* * *

The company, now known as Atlantic Industrial, includes Atlantic Scaffolding, a high-performance scaffolding contractor that specializes in critical path turnaround projects, cat cracker turnarounds and boiler outages at power plants and paper mills; and Atlantic Plant Services, which provides scaffolding services to the refining and petrochemical, power, pulp and paper, and manufacturing sectors nationwide. Atlantic recently acquired Insulco, a provider of comprehensive insulation services, including installation, removal and replacement, and insulation material distribution based in Joliet, Ill. The company also offers a proprietary scaffold management software information system called DSMS™ that provides clients with unrivaled management control with its cost-accounting and planning data, tracking capabilities, and invoicing data.

Vrettakos credits the company's success to its strong, experienced team of managers and employees, its remarkable safety record and its use of new technology in staying competitive in the industry.

"I'm very proud that our company is attractive enough as an opportunity for people of this caliber to come and work for us," Vrettakos said of his management team. "Craig Kaple, who is the president of Atlantic Scaffolding, and Darryl Schimeck, president of Atlantic Plant Services, each have over 20 years of experience in industrial services. Both are guys of good character, and I'm very proud to have them as executives."

Joe Williams remains with Atlantic Industrial as a vice president and a shareholder. The management team also includes Director of Environmental, Safety and Health Barry Guidry, who Vrettakos credits with elevating Atlantic's safety culture from "good" to "great," and Vice President of Business Development Scott Thibodeaux.

"We also have a lot of good regional managers around the country," Vrettakos said. "We have a fantastic team."

Future chapters in the Atlantic Industrial tale remain to be written as the company expands into new geographic regions and segments of business. For now, the Atlantic team — now approximately 1,600 strong — will continue to offer its bundle of services to customers seeking quality, safety, efficiency and ver-

Vrettakos credits Atlantic Industrial's success to its strong, experienced team of managers and employees, its remarkable safety record and its use of new technology in staying competitive in the industry.

satility, aiming high just as Vrettakos did during his first years in the business.

When asked if there is a true formula for success for young workers dreaming of achieving great heights in the scaffolding industry or any other, Vrettakos is quick to emphasize the basics of running a business.

"Knowing what I've learned in the last few years, I would say it's important to get some formal education," Vrettakos said. "You can't build your whole business around the technical skills you learn as a tradesman. And if I could do it over again, I would have hired a CPA when the company was a year old instead of 10 to help us with the administrative side of the business. You can get a lot farther a lot faster if your business is well rounded and not just operationally focused."

Inner strength, however, is more vital than education, according to Vrettakos.

"It is essential to be passionate about what you are doing," he said. "You need lots of drive to overcome the hurdles. And you don't have to be the smartest guy in the room, but you must be the most tenacious."

THE BIC ALLIANCE:
PAST, PRESENT AND FUTURE

The life of an entrepreneur is filled with big moments — in most cases, enough to fill a book. In 2005, BIC Alliance CEO and Founder Earl Heard proved that by publishing *It's What We Do Together That Counts: The BIC Alliance Story*, a story written to inspire others to work hard and overcome adversity in pursuit of their dreams.

Founded in Baton Rouge, La., in 1984, the BIC Alliance — publisher of the *Business & Industry Connection* (BIC), the nation's largest multi-industry, multidepartmental newsmagazine — is the product of Earl's vision of success as an entrepreneur. That dream, which carried him through the various highs and lows of entrepreneurship, began in Earl's childhood.

As a boy in the early '50s, Earl sold television schedules door-to-door in his neighborhood, sold soft drinks at Louisiana State University and high school football games, and mowed lawns using a lawnmower financed by his father. Selling soft drinks and TV schedules taught him the importance of managing his time and going the extra mile to be successful. At the football stadiums, for instance, spectators in the highest seats would pay Earl and his brother George the greatest tips for having climbed so far to serve them.

One of the prevailing themes of Earl's first book is the importance of being able to turn adversity into opportunity. Earl learned this on several different occasions during adolescence and early adulthood.

Around the age of 12, Earl began to frequent a public swimming pool in his neighborhood. Unlike the other children, however, he had never learned to swim. On many occasions, he had to be rescued by life-guards and other swimmers as he screamed and cried in fear of drowning. A helpful lifeguard named Freddie Marks then took him under his wing and taught him the fundamentals of swimming. Earl not only learned to swim, but he also went on to become a lifeguard. This experience marked the beginning of his lifelong interest in training.

Shortly after beginning his career with Ethyl Corp. as an operator at the age of 23, Earl witnessed an ethyl chloride plant explosion that ignited a fire. Earl had been loading a tank car a mile away from the explo-sion when it occurred, so he was in a position to fight the fire. Earl's supervisor, Frank Richardson, taught him how to cut off the fuel source of the fire rather than extinguishing it, which would have created a volatile vapor cloud.

The experiences in life-or-death situations gave Earl a new set of survival skills, including the ability to think three-dimensionally and make quick decisions. This would come in handy in the early '80s after he launched his first businesses — an industrial safety training video produc-tion company called Videoscan and *The Training Coordinator*, which was the first training magazine in the petroleum industry. (Earl gave up his career at Ethyl — where he had been promoted to training manager after 15 years on the job — to found Videoscan in 1980.) The video production company failed, but the concept of a multi-industry, multidepartmental publication was born, and *The Training Coordinator* would later evolve into BIC magazine.

After a brief stint working for Hill Petroleum in Krotz Springs, La., Earl launched two new publications — *The Woman's Coordinator* and *The Business & Industry Coordinator*. While selling advertising for *The Woman's Coordinator*, Earl was inspired by Baton Rouge businessman Guy Bellello to offer BIC's marketing partners the opportunity to sponsor the publication's front cover. (Bellello invested $5,000 to put his wife on the cover of *The Woman's Coordinator*.) The idea could not have come at a better time — BIC was in the introductory stage of the product life cycle, and its future was uncertain.

Earl remained confident in the niche he'd carved for the publication in its formative stages. Unlike most industry publications, BIC was horizontal and reached a wide variety of industries, allowing marketing partners to target a wider audience for a comparatively small investment. BIC also offered its partners the opportunity to use the publication as a third-party newsletter and its database for prospecting, and provided editorial and ad design services and direct mail to key clients and prospects. The concept was new in the '80s and is still unique within the publishing industry.

With the help of family, friends and colleagues in business, Earl was able to secure the resources necessary to turn his new business model into a formula for success, though it would take many years of hard work, determination and prayer to reach the light at the end of the tunnel.

* * *

From day one, the BIC Alliance has been run like a family rather than a business owned by a family. Earl and his wife, Mary Alice "Bodi" Heard, view the BIC staff members as sons and daughters, and they're proud to admit it.

It's only fitting that the future of the company is in the hands of someone who is both a member of the Heards' family and a partner in their business.

In the late '80s, Earl's daughter Dane began dating Thomas Brinsko, an LSU law student from Mandeville, La. When Earl and Thomas first met, the former was living in a modest apartment in Baton Rouge that he was renting on trade for advertising in BIC magazine.

It had been a full seven years since Earl's first businesses collapsed, but he was still working day and night to try to build BIC into a profitable venture. Swimming in debt, he spent nearly all of his time managing editorial content for BIC and driving to and from Houston to network with prospective clients in order to show the benefactors who supported him financially and the loved ones who prayed for him that he possessed the will to succeed again. Although many individuals stepped up to the plate in that regard, Earl was perhaps the only person who knew without a shadow of a doubt that he would survive and prosper. To Earl, failure was not an option.

For Thomas, the way forward seemed much clearer. Like Earl, he spent most of his time working to secure a stable future. As a student of LSU's Paul M. Hebert Law Center, Thomas was in constant competition with his peers. This was something of a culture shock for Thomas, who had earned a bachelor's degree in general business from the University of Southwestern Louisiana (now the University of Louisiana-Lafayette), where camaraderie and mutual support were virtues among students.

For the first year or so, he struggled to work his way out of the bottom half of his class ranking. But as the son of a painting contractor and the grandson of a successful airplane manufacturer and a delicatessen owner, Thomas had inherited a strong work ethic. He pushed harder in his studies than he ever had before, and went on to graduate in the top third of his class in 1991.

Though they were bound by the burgeoning relationship between Dane and Thomas, who were married in 1990, the two men were on very different courses in their lives. After Thomas received his juris doctorate, he accepted a job offer from Exxon and went to work as a petroleum land-man in Houston. Even though the new job forced the Brinskos to live in a strange place miles away from their families, the idea of working for a large and prestigious company in a major metropolitan area exhilarated Thomas. He hit the ground running, making a name for himself not only within his department but also in professional associations related to the industry.

Meanwhile, Earl had begun to make great strides in his effort to establish the BIC Alliance as a primary network for communication between buyers and suppliers in the energy industries. The company hosted a series of trade shows and networking events across the Gulf South that attracted who's who in business and industry. Industrial service companies began to see greater value in sponsoring major marketing campaigns in BIC magazine, and advertising revenues began to increase. That allowed Earl to bring in a diverse staff of talented production and sales team members, who took some of the burden of maintaining BIC's success off his shoulders, though he continued to work hard generating new business, networking with clients and training his people.

Despite the divergence of their career paths, Earl and Thomas had flirted with the idea of working together from the beginning. Their first professional interaction, which occurred while Thomas was still at LSU, resulted from an act of betrayal that shocked Earl and threatened to destroy his faith in other people.

It was discovered around 1989 that an old friend Earl had hired to manage the finances of the BIC Alliance had been siphoning funds and using the money to pay for an expensive apartment and his daughter's college tuition. Earl enlisted the help of Thomas, who knew a little about legal matters related to embezzlement, to develop a restitution plan for repayment of the $20,000 that had been stolen. The money was never repaid in full, but out of the incident came the mutual realization that Earl

"Our commitment to faith, hard work and perseverance has brought us success beyond our wildest dreams, and we are forever thankful to God, our families, our team members, and all of our BIC Alliance partners"

— Earl Heard

and Thomas made a great team. Thomas began to do part-time jobs for the company, including payroll, distribution of magazines and classified ad sales. Energetic, thorough and possessing a knack for organization, he made a big impression on Earl and the other BIC Alliance team members.

* * *

Although Thomas could very well have taken a full-time job at the BIC Alliance upon finishing law school, the offer from Exxon was just too sweet to pass up.

"I liked Earl, but I certainly didn't love him the way I do now," Thomas said. "I didn't want my first job to be with the family business, and he felt the same way. He knew I'd do better going somewhere else and possibly working for him at some time in the future. We agreed to leave that door open."

Even as he began his new career, Thomas stayed in close contact with his father-in-law, who had a wealth of experience in the energy industry. For Thomas, picking Earl's brain for valuable lessons about working in the world of industry was common sense, even though times had changed greatly since Earl left Ethyl Corp. in 1980.

"I would take vacation days from Exxon to attend trade shows with Earl and keep a pulse on what he was doing," Thomas said. "I'd get lots of attention when I'd walk into his hospitality events wearing my Exxon name badge. It was a lot of fun, and a great learning experience."

After spending two years in Houston, Thomas jumped at the chance to transfer to Exxon's New Orleans office. The move brought him and Dane closer to their families and gave Earl and Thomas more time to spend sharing ideas and encouraging one another.

By the late '90s, Thomas's reputation at Exxon had grown so much that he began to draw interest from a number of companies looking to hire him away. His satisfaction and job security kept him from pursuing other opportunities until 1997, when an exploration and production company located just across the street from Exxon called. Denver-based Key Production Co. had recently launched its Gulf Coast division in New Orleans and had a position available for a landman. Key offered Thomas a salary that was significantly higher than what he had been making, along with a degree of autonomy that could not be achieved at Exxon, where all decisions were made by committee.

"I went to my boss at Exxon and said, 'I'm not really interested in leaving, but there's a chance for me to make this much money,'" Thomas said. "I told him I'd be more than happy to stay if they could come within a certain dollar amount of the offer. And he just said, 'Congratulations! I'd love to keep you, but you need to go and make that money.'"

Thomas describes his stint with Key as one of the most enjoyable periods of his career. For the first time, he was empowered to make decisions that impacted his company. Thomas and his Key teammates — two geologists and an engineer, initially — turned a $20 million exploration budget allocation into great yields of oil and gas. Thomas received huge bonuses in return for his hard work, and with a wife and a two-year-old daughter named Hannah Yvonne at home and another baby on the way, things couldn't have been better for him professionally or personally.

In August 1997, however, a single incident changed the lives of the Heard and Brinsko families forever. While on a trip to Houston, Earl was brutally attacked by three men who only spared his life through an arbitrary decision and stole his car. To this day, Earl credits God for giving him the strength to find his way to a hospital before he bled to death.

The recovery period put him out of commission for several months. Although his staff was very capable of running the BIC Alliance in his absence, Earl, who was 55 years of age at the time, decided that the company needed another strong leader to fill the void in the event that he could no longer do so.

Earl made an offer to Thomas to join the BIC Alliance with the understanding that he could evolve into the role of company president and chief operating officer when the time came for Earl to enter semi-retirement. In April 1999, Thomas accepted the offer, left his job at Key, and moved his family to Baton Rouge.

For the Brinsko family, leaving the security of Key was a tough decision. Perhaps their desire to ensure a successful future for the family business was the only factor that could have pulled them away from such a great situation. According to Thomas, however, the idea of truly becoming a leader for the first time in his career was very appealing.

"I thought of all the things I enjoyed about working at Key," Thomas said. "And I decided that it wasn't so much the oil and gas exploration as it was the autonomy and authority. I knew that if I went to work with Earl and became president of the company, I'd have even more power to make decisions. I was also excited about being a part of the BIC Alliance's mission to connect business and industry for the betterment of all."

A large portion of Thomas's first year at BIC was spent learning the company's processes and observing the way Earl worked.

"I didn't want to do anything but carry Earl's briefcase at first," Thomas said. "I had been in industry for a while, but BIC was focused on a wide variety of industries, including refining and chemical, and I had always worked on the exploration and production side. So I spent a lot of time in his office just listening to his sales presentations and his conversations with clients."

Thomas had never been a salesman, but through constant interaction with BIC Alliance marketing partners and prospects, he developed the customer service orientation that would allow him to grow into that role. He also began to work closely with the people who managed the BIC Alliance's production and administration divisions in order to fully understand how they made their decisions and managed their daily tasks.

By 2002, Thomas had established a level of comfort in managing all aspects of the business. In April of that year, Earl appointed him president and COO, and announced that Thomas would henceforth be responsible for the day-to-day responsibilities of the BIC Alliance while Earl himself would move into the role of chief executive and gradually decrease his workload. A year later, Thomas and Dane agreed to return to Houston to oversee the BIC Alliance's Western United States operation and network more closely with industry-related associations in Texas. (In 2006, Thomas was elected to the board of directors of the Texas Chemical Council/Association of the Chemical Industry in Texas.)

In the past eight years, Earl and Thomas, along with their gifted and hardworking sales, production and administrative team members, have steered the company toward unprecedented success. BIC magazine has been firmly established as the nation's largest multi-industry, multidepartmental publication. Ind-Viro Search, a merger-and-acquisition matchmaking and executive recruiting firm launched in 1997, has become a trusted source through which buyers, sellers and investors of energy-, construction- and environmental-related companies can connect with one another. BIC Publishing, the BIC Alliance's custom book publishing division, released *It's What We Do Together That Counts* in 2005 and *Energy Entrepreneurs, Vol. 1* in 2007 and expects to produce one or two similar publications by 2009.

"Our commitment to faith, hard work and perseverance has brought us success beyond our wildest dreams, and we are forever thankful to God, our families, our team members, and all of our BIC Alliance partners," Earl said.

* * *

On the surface, Earl and Thomas are quite different, but their strengths are well-matched. Earl is a visionary — he possesses the ability to see potential in any given situation and motivate the right people to help him bring his ideas into action. Thomas is an implementer — he has a special talent for assessing a problem or an objective and creating the most efficient and successful way to arrive at a solution given the time and resources available. As their working relationship has evolved, they've influenced one another in many ways.

"Watching Earl has been very educational for me and made me realize what my challenges are," Thomas said. "I don't think of myself as an entrepreneur, but there are areas in which I'm trying to grow so that I may become more like one."

Indeed, Thomas doesn't carry the old entrepreneurial burden of creating something out of nothing because it's already been done. He is, however, responsible for carrying on Earl's tradition of maintaining the success of the BIC Alliance by treating clients and employees as partners, staying on top of industry news and trends, generating new business through networking, and investing resources in ways that consistently improve BIC magazine and the different services the company offers. That hasn't been difficult for Thomas, who considers it all a labor of love.

"Earl likes to say that I enjoy selling more than I do getting paid for what I sell," Thomas said. "But I really do enjoy my work. It's easy for me to say that because I make a good living, but I don't work to make a lot of money. I work to make a living for my family and to help strengthen the connection between business and industry in America."

Thomas and Dane now have three young children — Hannah, Mary and Michael — and are enjoying life in Houston. It would appear that Thomas's career has come full circle, but he feels as though his metamorphosis from an up-and-coming landman at Exxon to the future patriarch of the BIC Alliance has been a long process of maturation, both professional and spiritual.

"I've changed a lot as a person, and that may be just a part of getting older," Thomas said. "But I realize more and more that even those who don't believe in God know that the principles taught in the Bible are true. Some of them might make little sense to us on the surface, like the idea that it's better to give than to receive. You ask yourself, 'What does that really mean?' But when you truly give to someone, you are rewarded and you feel good."

The Heards and Brinskos believe that families who pray and play together, stay together. Shown here are Earl and Bodi Heard and Thomas, Dane, Hannah, Mary and Michael Brinsko, aboard a Disney cruise in 2007.

Thomas believes that faith and fatherhood have allowed him to retain a certain sense of humility he feels is important to running a successful business.

"When you have children, you learn they have different personalities," Thomas said. "Some children have to be disciplined in order to get them to listen, but others only need a stern glance. The Bible teaches that we're all God's children, and I feel that I'm the child who only needs a stern glance. The more I cling to God's teachings, the easier my life is. I'll never knowingly deceive someone, and if I make a mistake, I try to own it right away. No one's perfect, least of all me."

He does, however, believe that the BIC Alliance team is pretty close. He takes special pride in the fact that the company is being run by a group that strives for excellence, from top to bottom. This only makes it easier for him to do his job and for Earl to focus on the things he enjoys the most.

"People sometimes say that Earl will never really retire," Thomas said. "But to me, he is retired. He's phased himself out of the BIC Alliance's day-to-day operations, but he's still around to make key decisions, develop long-term strategies and watch what's going on.

"The goal of retirement is to put yourself in a position to do whatever you want to do," he continued. "I think Earl gets more pleasure from publishing books about entrepreneurs, delivering his Alligator Management & Marketing seminars and keynote presentations, attending trade shows, doing benevolent work, and helping people in business and

184

industry to grow in their professional and personal lives than he would from, say, playing golf."

The BIC Alliance is poised to further its success in the years to come. While Earl and Thomas both know that challenges lie around every corner, they are secure in the belief that they have the right system in place to overcome adversity.

They've also proven that you don't necessarily have to share a bloodline to work toward common dreams.

50 TIPS FOR SUCCESS IN ENTREPRENEURSHIP

BY EARL HEARD

1. Join and become active in the organizations related to your profession.
2. Focus on being more interested instead of being more interesting.
3. Treat others as you would like to be treated instead of treating them the way they treat you.
4. Learn and practice the art of listening.
5. More people become successful because they're nice than because they're brilliant
6. First impressions are important — we never get a second chance to make one.
7. Keep good business and personal financial records.
8. Save regularly. It's not how much you earn that counts, it's how much you've got when you need it.
9. Learn and practice the art of networking by making three excellent referrals per day.
10. Keep a business journal and a family journal and review them regularly.
11. When mistakes happen, learn from them.
12. Don't be afraid of hard work. It won't kill you.
13. Set written business and personal goals — daily, weekly, monthly and annually.
14. If you supervise others, know and review their goals at least monthly.
15. Practice what you preach. No one likes a hypocrite.
16. Practice safety and environmental consciousness on the job and off.
17. Become a positive role model at work and at home.
18. Before speaking, think about how the person listening will interpret what you say.
19. Encourage others instead of putting them down.

20. Never stop learning. The more we learn, the more we earn.
21. Don't discriminate toward others on the basis of race, color, religion or economic status.
22. Seek mentors for yourself and become a mentor to others.
23. Listen to motivational speakers, tapes, preachers, etc.
24. Learn and practice effective time management techniques.
25. Learn how to dress and dine properly.
26. Learn and practice good verbal communication skills.
27. Thank people regularly for their business, help, etc.
28. Surround yourself with honest, ethical and hardworking people.
29. Stay away from negative people, places and situations.
30. Before you evaluate others, ask them to evaluate their own performance.
31. Build a library of motivational/how-to books and magazines and read them.
32. Practice self control in all that you say and do.
33. Practice presentations before making them. A great way to do this is to videotape yourself making a presentation or watch yourself in a mirror acting as both the buyer and the seller.
34. When speaking or making a presentation, be prepared for anything or any question that might arise.
35. Research and prospecting are the keys to successful entrepreneurship and sales.
36. It's not "see more and you'll sell more" — it's more about prospecting better and then seeing more of the best prospects.
37. Remember what it was like at the bottom, and help others reach the next rung on the ladder of success.
38. It is more blessed to give than to receive.
39. Remember, Abe Lincoln lost many elections before becoming a winner. Never give up!
40. Learn to master nonverbal communication to influence others — facial expressions, tone of voice, listening, etc. Since 90 percent of our communication is nonverbal, it's important to remember that actions speak louder than words.

41. Preview before you begin a meeting, and review after you finish a meeting.
42. It's just as easy to sell a Rolls-Royce as it is a Chevrolet. You just don't have to sell as many of them!
43. One of the great things about starting at the bottom is that there is plenty of room to advance.
44. It's better to be perceived as a fool than to open your mouth and leave no doubt.
45. Compromise is better than confrontation. Find the middle ground where everyone is comfortable.
46. True success comes when we've reached the point where we are more concerned with doing what's right than obtaining money, publicity and/or recognition.
47. Before we can manage others effectively, we must master self-management.
48. The best way to build self-confidence is to know how to act properly and say the right things at the right time.
49. Attitude is more important than aptitude in determining altitude.
50. Remember — it's what we do together that counts!

SUGGESTED READING

-The Bible

-*The Entrepreneur's Creed: The Principles and Passions of 20 Successful Entrepreneurs*, by Merrill Oster and Mike Hamel

-*Halftime: Changing Your Game Plan from Success to Significance*, by Bob Buford

-*It's What We Do Together That Counts: The BIC Alliance Story*, by Earl Heard

-*Anatomy of an Entrepreneur: The Story of Joseph Jacobs, Founder of Jacobs Engineering*, by Joseph J. Jacobs

-*Nuts!: Southwest Airlines' Crazy Recipe for Business and Personal Success*, by Kevin Freiberg and Jackie Freiberg

-*Split Second Choice: The Power of Attitude*, by Jim Winner

-*Who Moved My Cheese?*, by Spencer Johnson, M.D.

-*Walt Disney: An American Original*, by Bob Thomas

-*The Prize: The Epic Quest for Oil, Money & Power*, by Daniel Yergin

-*Minute Motivators for Leaders*, by Stan Tolar

-How to Become CEO: The Rules for Rising to the Top of Any Organization, by Jeffrey J. Fox

-Onassis: Aristotle and Christina, by L.J. Davis

-Trump: The Art of the Deal, by Tony Schwartz

-Iacocca: An Autobiography, by Lee Iacocca with William Novak

-Entrepreneur Magazine's 303 Marketing Tips, by Rieva Lesonsky and Leann Anderson

-E Myth Mastery: The Seven Essential Disciplines for Building a World Class Company, by Michael E. Gerber

-The E Myth Revisited: Why Most Small Businesses Don't Work and What to Do About It, by Michael E. Gerber

-Dare to Lead: Proven Principles of Effective Leadership, by Byrd Baggett

-Maximizing Misfortune: Turning Life's Failures Into Success, by Jerome Edmondson

-Prosperity: The Choice is Yours, by Kenneth Copeland

-In Search of Excellence: Lessons from America's Best-Run Companies, by Thomas J. Peters and Robert H. Waterman

-A Hand to Guide Me, by Denzel Washington

-*7 Secrets of Great Entrepreneurial Masters: The Gem Power Formula for Lifelong Success*, by Allen E. Fishman

-*Women Entrepreneurs Only: 12 Women Entrepreneurs Tell the Stories of Their Success*, by Gregory K. Ericksen

-*If at First You Don't Succeed: The Eight Patterns of Highly Effective Entrepreneurs*, by Brent Bowers

-*The Entrepreneur Next Door: Discover the Secrets to Financial Independence*, by Bill Wagner

-*Entrepreneurship for Dummies*, by Kathleen Allen, Ph.D

-*The Spirit to Serve: Marriott's Way*, by J.W. Marriott Jr. and Kathi Ann Brown

-*Nothing Ventured Nothing Gained*, by Roger Fritz

WHAT'S NEXT?

Now that you've read these stories of modern-day heroes who have achieved success through faith, hard work and perseverance, what's next for you?

I learned long ago that knowledge alone is not enough. It's what we do with it that determines how successful we will be. Since today is the first day in the rest of our lives, I suggest you review the lessons learned from these stories and jot them down. (It's been said that the act of writing something down makes us 25 percent more likely to remember it.)

Personally, I like to read a book and then re-read it with a yellow highlighter in hand to mark the things that I want to remember. Next, I write those things down in a place where I can easily refer to them in the future. Once you've written down the key points you want to remember, I suggest you list your personal goals, along with an action plan.

I've found that reading the Bible and feeding my constant desire to learn and grow make each day an exciting and rewarding adventure. My favorite Bible verses are Matthew 7:7-8, which read, "Ask and it will be given to you, seek and you will find, knock and the door will be opened to you. For everyone who asks receives, he who seeks finds, and to those who knock, the door will be answered."

I've believed in God since I was a youth, but I became a born-again Christian after my near-death experience in 1997. I asked for God's forgiveness, and received it. I found the peace that I'd been seeking and the doors to success and happiness I'd been knocking on for years began to open wider than I'd ever dreamed they would. I learned firsthand that we can't outgive God, and we'll find the peace, happiness and success we seek if we put His teachings into action and knock upon His door.

Think of all these things, along with the wisdom of the people featured in this book, as you take that first step in the exciting journey toward greater success on the job and off.

— Earl Heard

NOTES

NOTES

NOTES

NOTES

CONTACT INFORMATION

Listed on the following pages is the contact information for the companies operated by the individuals featured in this book. Please contact them if you are interested in learning about their products and services.

Aimm Technologies
Phone: (409) 945-5414
Fax: (409) 945-6022
www.aimmtechnologies.com

Atlantic Industrial
Phone: (410) 799-0304
Fax: (410) 799-3435
Web Address: www.atlanticii.com

Empire Scaffold
Phone: (225) 272-6230
Fax: (225) 272-6212
Web Address: www.empirescaffold.com

Evergreen Industrial Services LLC
Phone: (281) 478-5800
Fax: (281) 478-5004
Web Address: www.evergreenics.com

FabEnCo Inc.
Phone: (713) 686-6620
Fax: (713) 688-8031
Web Address: www.safetygate.com

Glove Guard LP

Phone: (281) 426-2714
Fax: (281) 426-6135
Web Address: www.gloveguard.com

Godwin Pumps

Phone: (856) 467-3636
Fax: (856) 467-4428
Web Address: www.godwinpumps.com

Growth Capital Partners

Phone: (281) 445-6611
Fax: (281) 445-4298
Web Address: www.growth-capital.com

HRI Inc.

Phone: (417) 345-8019
Fax: (417) 345-8398
Web Address: www.hightempinc.com

Hub City Industries/Turbine Stimulation Technologies

Phone: (337) 706-1700
Fax: (337) 984-3868
Web Address: www.hubcityindustries.com or
www.turbinestimulationtechnologies.com

Keith Huber Inc.

Phone: (800) 33-HUBER [334-8237]
Fax: (228) 832-2068
Web Address: www.keithhuber.com

Louisiana CSI LLC

Phone: (225) 343-9125
Fax: (225) 388-9064
Web Address: www.la-csi.com

NLB Corp.
Phone: (248) 624-5555
Fax: (248) 624-0908
Web Address: www.nlbcorp.com

Plant Machine Works
Phone: (225) 775-7163
Fax: (225) 775-2743
Web Address: www.plantmachineworks.com

Repcon Inc.
Phone: (361) 289-6342
Fax: (361) 289-6389
Web Address: www.repconinc.com

Southland Fire & Safety Equipment Inc.
Phone: (225) 621-3473
Fax: (225) 621-3490
Web Address: www.southlandfire.com

Sparkling Clear Industries
Phone: (713) 956-8900
Fax: (713) 956-5237
Web Address: www.sparklingclear.com

SSCI-Environmental
Phone: (281) 486-1943
Fax: (281) 486-7415
Web Address: www.sscienvironmental.com

Turner Industries
Phone: (225) 922-5050
Fax: (225) 922-5055
Web Address: www.turner-industries.com

205